PATH TO ABUNDANT LIVING

CALVIN LIPSCOMB, CFP®, EA

PATH TO ABUNDANT LIVING

FINANCIAL TRUTHS
for CHRISTIANS

Advantage®

Published by Advantage, Charleston, South Carolina.
Member of Advantage Media Group.

ADVANTAGE is a registered trademark, and the Advantage colophon is a trademark of Advantage Media Group, Inc.

Printed in the United States of America.

10 9 8 7 6 5 4 3 2 1

ISBN: 978-1-59932-868-3
LCCN: 2017945543

Cover and layout design by Megan Elger.

To Donnamarie, thank you for your unwavering support.

ACKNOWLEDGMENTS

I want to first acknowledge the Lord for guiding and leading me to write this book to be a blessing to all believers who have taken the time to read it.

I want to thank the entire Advantage team for helping me bring this book from paper to print.

Thank you, Bob Sheasley, for sharing your faith, prayers, and talent in shaping a book that can guide all believers to the abundant living as promised by Scripture.

TABLE OF CONTENTS

A WORD FROM THE AUTHOR

THE ALMIGHTY'S DOLLARS

In God's perfect timing, and for his purposes, he arranged the flow of events so that I could write this book. I wish to open with a prayer that what I have written here is pleasing to him and that you, the readers, gain from these words the messages that he wants to impart about the biblical foundations of financial wisdom.

Out of disappointment, the Lord created opportunity. I had been anticipating an imminent contract to provide financial planning services for local military personnel, and I was excited about the prospect of helping them in a very real way. And then it all fell through. The job was to have started in January, and it was around Christmastime that I got the call—the contract had been pulled. "But we have something for you way upstate," I was told. On such short notice, and with family obligations, I felt that I had no choice but to decline, and I confess that I was letting it get me down.

Then my phone rang. "I need help," said the caller, who introduced himself as Bervon. "My life is a mess." I listened as he told me a bit of his story. He had been a Christian for all his thirty-five years, he said, and was involved with the church, but he was having some serious money issues. "Can we get together as soon as possible and talk for a while?" he asked.

"Sure," I said. "We can do that. May I ask why it was me you chose to call?" He didn't seem to have a specific answer, other than that he had heard that I offered financial planning services and that for some reason he just felt that I was the one he should reach out to. "I just felt drawn to you," he said.

We arranged for me to visit his house a few days later to chat, and I showed up at the appointed time. Bervon looked surprised when he answered my knock. His wife had fallen ill the day before, and he had tried to leave me a message canceling our meeting. For whatever reason, I didn't get that message. I try to be conscientious about checking my voicemail, but I either overlooked his message or it went astray somehow.

"I guess I could talk for five minutes since you're here anyway," he said. An hour later, we were still deep in conversation. I cannot help but think, in retrospect, that I wasn't meant to get that voicemail. This was a man who needed my perspective. He needed the sympathetic ear of someone who understood, from real-life experience, the mistakes he was making and how he could rise above them.

I listened as Bervon told me what he was going through. It's not my purpose here to relate those details, other than to say that he didn't want to make the same mistakes that his father, who also was struggling financially, had repeatedly made. He wanted to turn matters around before it was too late. I assured him that it wasn't too late and that I, too, had encountered tough times on my journey to financial success.

"Let me ask you something," I said, as we neared the end of our talk. "As a fellow Christian, do you feel that the church did a very good job of teaching you the basics of how to manage money?"

"No, I can't say I learned much at all there," he answered. "In fact, I really didn't hear it from anyone."

In my observation, I must say that he is not alone in that regard. A lot of people in the church are hurting financially, and the lack of education and awareness is at the root of the problem. People cling to myths, believing in them even when those myths are averse to God's truth, and that's what keeps them down. That is what keeps them from growing into mighty men and women of wealth who might otherwise do so much for God's kingdom.

Nobody in the church had told Bervon, or me, what we needed to know to thrive, and that is the case for countless other Christians. Instead, people are left to shape their beliefs and attitudes on the prevailing "wisdom" that they pick up from worldly sources. For example: "It takes money to make money." That is a falsehood that deadens their ambition to do better. Feeling that it would be futile, they don't even try to set aside anything for the future. *Why bother to save just $50 or $100 a month*, they tell themselves, *if it's never going to amount to anything?* Let me be clear: it can and it will amount to much.

And sometimes, as we will see, Christians hold tight to one biblical verse or another without examining the greater context regarding God's clear instructions for financial responsibility. Knowing that the Lord provides for us does not mean we can just lay back and do nothing. He provides us with tools to do his work, and he expects us to pick them up and use them.

Bervon wasn't in a position that day to pay me for my services, but God had positioned both of us. Bervon needed some direction, but I, too, needed some direction. After meeting with Bervon, I knew in my heart that it was no coincidence that this man, this fellow believer in Christ, had happened upon my name and called me, out of all the financial planners that he might have contacted for assistance. I also knew that it was no coincidence that my contract with the military had been canceled, opening a hole in my schedule. The Lord had provided both the opportunity and the incentive for me to get moving on something to serve his greater purpose. Although losing that contract had felt like a door of opportunity was closing on me, the Lord opened another door for me to walk through. God has a way of doing that.

For years, I had recognized that the church had not been teaching biblical principles for managing money. So what was I going to do about it? Just complain? Just sit back and figure that God would do something about it in his own time? Well, God was doing something about it. It was time, and he wanted to use me as an instrument for change. As I offered Bervon some guidance that day, I kept thinking that so many others needed to hear those clear principles. Later, as I reviewed our conversation, I thought, *Now is the time. This is the time for me to write down these truths, from God's holy perspective. This is my opportunity to write a book about fundamental finances for Christians.*

I had been helping individuals to understand how to better manage and grow their money. That way, they could become not only better providers for their families but also better stewards for a world in need. A Good Samaritan with financial means, after all, can give back far more than one without. My financial advice, however, was reaching people one at a time. While working with clients, I had often felt that having a book to offer them would magnify the power of our one-on-one sessions. A book could disseminate God's financial principles to a much wider audience.

And that was my motivation for writing this book and getting it published. God not only brought Bervon to me to help clarify that mission but also cleared the way so that I would be better able to focus on it. Had it not been for the Lord's intervention, this book would not be in print today.

Money is not ungodly, as some people have been led to believe. What is ungodly is the love of money—the worship of the mighty dollar. Since the Lord is the source of all that we have, you can think of that money instead as the Almighty's dollars—and he expects them to be put to good use. Paul was able to spread the gospel because good people of wealth and means were able to send money to support him. The Lord does not expect us to give away every cent. He expects us to wisely save and multiply our money so that we may build greater resources to do his work.

I grew up in church, but nobody there told me that financial success depends upon living within your means. Nobody told me about the power of saving and compounding through the years. The church teaches us so many important things about how to live, so why does it not teach about good financial practices? If we believe that the Bible is our guide for living, then it follows that we should also consider it to be our guide in obtaining financial abundance.

God desires that we should live abundantly, which is why he has provided the tools, if we choose to use them. We should be active Christians, not passive ones. We should step forward to make things happen, for ourselves, our families, our communities, our world, our God. Through him, all things are possible.

Although this book takes a Christian perspective, I do not limit my practice to working only with fellow believers. I recognize that we have a diversity of people all around us with different religions and creeds, but I believe that truth is universal—and as I relate those universal truths, I must be true to my own beliefs. I want to share who I am, and faith in Christ is central to that. It is the essence of my heart and soul, and nothing can separate me from that.

A native of Brooklyn, New York, I was deeply involved in the church during my formative years, from age twelve into the young adulthood of my midtwenties. During that time, I was involved in church virtually every day, and that certainly should have prepared me for life. Then, as I got older, I found my finances were in a mess. It seemed I had not been prepared for all aspects of life, and I drifted away for a time when the storms of life happened, as they will. Lacking a full foundation that included financial wisdom, I felt disillusioned. I felt that the church had let me down. But the Lord had never let me down, and he was there to pick me up and keep me on his path.

As a Certified Financial Planner™, I have met many people who lack the needed financial knowledge, tools, and plan to meet their stated life goals. After working together I was able to fit all of the elements of their lives together into a comprehensive financial action plan. As a tax preparer years ago, I began meeting people in need. When you see a client's tax return, you see his or her financial life laid out as an open book right in front of you. I saw the tax consequences of inadequate planning and poor decisions. I saw how badly people needed guidance, and I also saw that they were not getting it. That is why I resolved to expand my horizons to become a Certified Financial Planner™ practitioner.

I offer true comprehensive planning, emphasizing the social element. My philosophy is to work with the people first, not the money first. No matter your stage in life, and no matter what the state of your finances, you need a financial plan. If you are young, you need to set things in order so that you can build toward a productive future. If you are on the verge of retirement, you need to get all the pieces into place so that you have an income sufficient for the rest of your life and a solid estate plan for your heirs. If you are in-between, you need guidance on which financial tools you should be using to maximize savings and growth.

The goal of this book is to speak to people of all ages. Whatever your age, this book is for you and for those in your life whom you care about. Your concerns will differ depending upon your stage of life, but this much is the same: you need to plan it out carefully, and you need to do it God's way so that you will be prepared to fulfill whatever purpose he assigns you. He expects his children to reach out into the world. As you turn these pages, I hope to equip you with the financial knowledge and the biblical principles that will enable you to help yourself and to help others.

INTRODUCTION

A FINANCIAL BLESSING

The Scriptures tell us that if people are to learn about Christ, somebody must teach them, for "how shall they hear without a preacher?" It's a truth that extends to many areas of life—including coming to see the light of financial security.

In this book, my goal is to empower you to be a financial blessing to you and your family, to your church, and to whomever and whatever else is important to you. I will do so by showing you the spiritual and scriptural foundation for financial prosperity.

I was exposed to the Scriptures from a young age—but that did not make me financially ready for life. I was not taught important life lessons about money. I did not get the knowledge and wisdom to become financially independent. When it came to money, I was not trained in the way I should go.

I have found that many Christians struggle economically because they are not financially aware or prepared. Are you? Did anyone teach you about money and its power? Though I did not get that instruction in childhood, I have learned much since—and in the pages ahead I will share with you what I have learned.

This is not a get-rich-quick book. I will not be showing you how to turn limited resources into an easy million. Could it happen? Yes. However, for the vast majority of people, it will not—so if that is what you are looking to do, you might want to read something else.

This book will focus instead on basic money principles for becoming financially independent. These principles are nothing fancy or flashy. They can help you no matter where you are financially or how much you earn or whether your financial goals are modest or ambitious.

Throughout the book, I will encourage you to take the time to reflect—to discover your thoughts and feelings about money and the "why" of how you use and manage your money. You need to look inward at your financial habits, motivations, and mind-set to take charge of your finances. I will also point out life problems and concerns that you must address. Those issues are interrelated and can help or hinder your finances. Nothing happens in a vacuum.

This journey of self-discovery will allow you to shake off the shackles of financial ignorance and overcome the despair of a debt-laden life. Using biblically based money principles, you can shine as a financial light at home, at work, and in the church.

I believe in tough love. "Thy rod and thy staff, they comfort me," David wrote in Psalm 23, acknowledging the need not only for guidance but also for discipline. I will be clear about how you can go astray financially. All my advice to you comes from a place of love—and a desire to help you avoid the mistakes that I made and to grow financially, no matter your circumstances or where you are in life.

CHAPTER 1

MASTER OF YOUR FINANCES

And Naomi had a kinsman of her husband's, a mighty man of wealth, of the family of Elimelech; and his name was Boaz.

—Ruth 2:1

The parable of the Good Samaritan is so powerful and widely preached that people around the world, Christian or not, understand the reference. The parable teaches us to show compassion to people in distress, even if they are not like us—and even if they would not have shown us such compassion. It's a lesson about giving and about loving your neighbor.

Do you truly know the nature of a Good Samaritan? In the biblical account in Luke 10, the Samaritan bound up the wounds of a traveler who had been beaten by robbers, took him to an inn, left money for his further care, and told the innkeeper that he would pay any bill that might remain. A number of people are willing to show such compassion and support, as you may be. But do you have the financial resources to do so? Can the Lord use you to be such a financial blessing?

It has been said that prayer alone will not fill an empty belly, clothe a naked body, or cure the sick and injured. In telling this parable, did Jesus say that the Samaritan prayed a mighty prayer and God healed the traveler? No, he said the Samaritan cleaned the man's wounds with wine and oil, personally escorted him to safety, and paid for his needs. The Samaritan took earthly, mundane action, driven by compassion and mercy.

He also had the means for it—he possessed the money to accomplish the task. Perhaps he had saved and invested wisely or succeeded in business. This we do know: the Samaritan had managed his financial affairs so that he was ready and able to act when the Lord moved him.

That is a key element that I overlooked for years, and it is a point often missed when teaching the parable: the Samaritan's financial house was in order, and the Lord was therefore able to use him as a blessing for someone in dire need. If you are broke, how can you be a financial blessing?

Are you ready to become a Good Samaritan?

In the Book of Ruth, we read about Ruth's faithfulness to Naomi and how it led to her marriage to Boaz, a righteous man. Through that union, Ruth became the great-grandmother of King David. We see how God makes a way.

We learn also that Boaz was "a mighty man of wealth," clearly an excellent man of business. The word *might*, especially in the Old Testament, often is used to mean physical strength and prowess. Here, it describes the might of Boaz's money, his economic strength and power. How else could he have purchased and redeemed the fields of Naomi? How else could he have married and provided for Ruth while taking on the financial responsibilities of caring for Naomi as well?

If he had not tended to his business, if he had squandered every dollar, could Boaz have become such a mighty man of wealth? If he had saved nothing, would he have had the resources to redeem the land of Naomi? To do what needed to be done, Boaz had to master his finances. The Lord did not come down from heaven to tell the leaders to give the land to Boaz, for Naomi's sake. He did, however, use Boaz and his wealth to make it happen. Boaz was in the right financial position to serve the Lord's purposes.

The Lord wants you to become a mighty person of wealth. He has ministries to furnish and lives to save, and he is looking for people of means to step forward. It takes time, hard work, discipline, and commitment—and you have made a great start by picking up and reading this book.

As I was writing this chapter, I received a phone call from a minister who needed to file some IRS forms for a nonprofit ministry that she was establishing. I raised a variety of concerns with her, explaining what needed to be done without delay so that her ministry would be spared unnecessary expenses. Potential donors to her ministry would expect that nonprofit status, of course—but she had not been prepared financially to set it up in a timely manner. The lack of money was holding back a ministry from reaching out to souls in need of Christ. She needed someone in her corner to help her become a mighty person of wealth.

Are you a master of your finances? You need to develop financial discipline so that you are prepared to do the work of the Lord. Your belief in Christ does not mean you will not have to deal with expenses and financial challenges. By facing them, you learn money management and how to be a good steward.

People tend to find the money for things that are important to them. They go on trips, enjoy nice meals, buy new cars and new clothes—and so if doing the Lord's work is important to them, they can find the money for that as well. The Good Samaritan did not ask the innkeeper to take care of the injured man for free. And Boaz got the money together to redeem the land of Naomi and came prepared to conduct business.

You, too, need to be prepared to do business. "It is more blessed to give than to receive," we read in Acts 20:35. I want you to be the blessed one giving to those around you.

THE BOTTOM LINE

The Lord wants you to become a mighty person of wealth. You need to develop financial discipline so that you are prepared to do his work.

CHAPTER 2

THE TRUTH ABOUT MONEY

And ye shall know the truth, and the truth shall make you free.

—John 8:32

True freedom comes from knowing Jesus, who brings truth into our lives. However, for your spiritual and earthly well-being, you also need money truths, financial truths, and economic truths.

Are you aware of key principles involving money? Do you share those truths with your family and other Christians? As you read this book, I want you to actively strive for deeper understanding, and pausing and answering these two questions is a good first step toward financial liberty.

We need to be set free. We must move from darkness to light. Financial debt and mismanagement keeps many people in bondage. Think about how money issues are troubling the life of someone you know—a friend, perhaps, or someone in your congregation or a member of your family. Maybe even you.

I think back on my own financial failures and how my lack of financial knowledge affected my emotional and psychological well-being. Today I make my living by helping people with their finances, but I was not always a finance person. Even after I became aware, I still had to deal with the consequences of past decisions. I still had to wrestle with my thoughts and attitudes about money. As I moved forward into the light, I still stumbled.

You, too, may well feel that way after reading this book, but do not let the past prevent you from advancing. You still may stumble as you regain your footing but not as frequently when you apply these principles. The problem isn't the stumbling; the problem is not getting back on your feet. If you fall, don't stay down.

SPIRITUAL MISCONCEPTIONS

We must start with some misplaced beliefs about Christian living and money. We must dispel some myths, some of which I once believed. You, too, may need to wake up to some truths—so let's take the time to expose these misconceptions. We must challenge ways of thinking that can hinder financial growth and prosperity.

"Money is evil."

Some people believe that you should not strive to be wealthy, but that is not the truth from Scripture. If you are happy with your economic situation, that is fine—but understand what the Bible actually says: "For the love of money is the root of all evil" (1 Timothy 6:10). Money is not the issue. Nothing is wrong with wanting money for things that are important. The issue is the love of money, the willingness to be deceitful and hurtful to get it.

Not every rich person is earthly minded, just as not every poor person is spiritual. Always remember that. You are not less spiritual because you desire and lead a life without money problems. You are not less spiritual if you become a person of means, as some Christians believe. Nor are you more spiritual if you are struggling to meet your monthly bills.

"It's okay to be poor."

The poor will always be among us, Jesus said. They can experience God's kingdom living within their circumstances—but that does not mean it is the will of God that every Christian be poor. You presumably are reading this book because you recognize that.

"I am come that they might have life, and that they might have it more abundantly," Jesus says in John 10:10. That is far from a mind-set of poverty, and yet many Christians hold on to the attitude that they should not pursue such abundance. Some wrongly believe that Jesus was only talking about internal abundance, but he came so that you might have external abundance, too. You can and you should strive for external abundance.

You are a child of the King. You should pursue better things in life—but financial prosperity will not just fall into your lap. You must work for it, and not everyone is willing to do what it takes. You would expect that Christians would be the best employees, with a strong work ethic, great customer service, and willingness to grow. Those are the characteristics that lead to career advancement along with financial gain—but how many of us exemplify those qualities in the workplace?

"God will just provide."

I have found that Christians often express that attitude to justify a lack of ambition and drive. Yes, God can and does provide, but does that mean that you do nothing? You should create the conditions and opportunities for God to provide.

"This we commanded you, that if any would not work, neither should he eat," Paul told the Thessalonians. That is the truth from God's word. You must not just lie back. You need to put forth real effort to change your financial situation.

"If the Lord is willing . . ."

I have often heard Christians preface their plans and expectations by referencing James 4:15: "For that ye ought to say, if the Lord will, we shall live, and do this, or that." Generally, they only cite the words "if the Lord will," but the verse is also saying that you should keep your commitments. God has given you breath for the day. Are you willing to do what needs to be done for the day?

The vast majority of people, whether they are believers or not, will not just wake up and be financially secure. They must take steps. They must do the work to make it happen. We read in Philippians 4:13: "I can do all things through Christ which strengthens me." The verse does not say that you will do all things or that you must do all things. You do have the power of choice, and for whatever reason, you may not be willing. Nor does the verse say that you are unable to do anything; it clearly says that through Christ, you can. You are able. The question is: Are you also willing? Are you committed and determined?

It is important to recognize these spiritual misconceptions that can keep you in financial bondage. The attitudes, beliefs, and feelings that influence your actions will prevent you from achieving financial abundance as written in God's word. Carefully consider the four attitudes that we just examined. If you are starting to feel uncomfortable, ask yourself why. I encourage you to get to the root of why you think the way you do. By doing so, you will be better able to become a blessing to those around you—family, friends, congregants, and, yes, strangers. You can be a vessel for those less fortunate.

As you strive to reach a higher financial purpose in life, you will feel as if you are climbing the rough side of the mountain. You will face temptations and distractions along your path. Jesus understood and withstood temptations, as we read in Matthew 4:1–10. He countered them with the power of the Scriptures. By understanding what God's word truly says about money and finances, you can be set free from the misinterpretations that will hold you back.

DISPELLING OTHER MYTHS

Let us look now at some other misconceptions that are not strictly Christian in their origin. I have observed the following attitudes among many people, including myself, which has a direct impact on their finances and life.

"I am too poor to save or invest."

No matter how little money you make, someone else will be making less than you—and finding a way to save something. Which clearly shows that you can, too. We will discuss how to do that later, but for now just know that you are able. You may be thinking it is easier said than done, and you are right, but are you going to let that stop you?

"I need a lot of money to invest."

For well over half my life, I believed this falsehood. The truth is that you do not need to start off with a lot of money. There are many investment and saving strategies by which you can grow your money starting with a small amount. A little bit of saving and investing over a long time will give you a lot in the end. We will explore this more later.

"The system is rigged for the rich."

The truly wealthy do have some advantages, but why would that stop everyone else from pursuing something better? If you cannot afford the type of home a billionaire could buy, does that mean you would not buy a home at all? The ultra-wealthy may have access to the ultimate in health care, but does that mean you will stop seeing your doctor? Of course not. Then why would you refrain from investing just because some others have much more to invest? Think hard on this one. This is one of the main reasons people do not start to invest.

"I can do this on my own."

Yes, you can, but then you probably are also reading books and articles, subscribing to newsletters, and sharing investment ideas with others, right? So you are not exactly

> a lone wolf. The vast majority of so-called do-it-yourself investors will seek help and guidance one way or another. However, I still find problems and weaknesses that need to be addressed when working with this group.

So many people make statements like those, and they often go unchallenged. Those are the underlying attitudes that will impact your financial and investment life in a negative way, regardless of your spiritual beliefs. Whether or not we recognize or acknowledge them, those attitudes, and others not mentioned, play a direct role in our moneymaking decisions.

Are any of those attitudes yours? Are you aware of these money beliefs influencing the way you manage your money? Do you see how the way you manage your money, based on those attitudes, impacts those around you? As you examine your values and beliefs about money and finance, always be aware of the myths so common in our society. You are on a quest for financial liberty. Falsehoods and half-truths will not set you free.

THE BOTTOM LINE

Money is not evil, despite what you might have been led to believe. That's not what Scriptures teach. It's time to dispel the many myths that discourage the creation of wealth that could do so much for God's kingdom, for you, and for your family.

CHAPTER 3

DEALING WITH DEBT

Owe no man anything, but to love one another.

—Romans 13:8

As a Christian, you no doubt will agree that you should be living by the Scriptures. Ask yourself, then, how close are you in practicing your biblical duty to be responsible for your debts. You must pay what you owe, or you should not borrow to begin with.

Debt will determine what you can and cannot do. It will determine how financially independent you can become. It will determine the extent to which you can support the ministry. That is why it is critical to manage it well. You have to learn to live with debt and use it wisely. You must never drown in it.

Some debts are good and can be profitable. Some debts are bad. And some are in the category of "*What was I thinking?!*" I have had all of those in the past—but too few of the good ones.

Dealing with debt effectively is the foundation of financial independence. Owing too much money will impact all your financial opportunities. If you have too much debt, you cannot save, invest, or become financially secure.

Let's say that you have monthly bills totaling $1,000 and that you have a monthly income of $1,000. What is your financial situation? Will you be able to save for anything? Will you be able to establish an emergency fund, which everyone should have? Unless you bring in more money than you pay out, you will not be able to do either. A thousand dollars minus a thousand dollars equals zero dollars.

It's an elementary equation, but many people do not seem to get it. I have worked with people with an income of $250,000 a year who were broke. Others earn $30,000 and have $10,000 in the bank. Unless you learn the discipline of saving, you can end up just spending more as you earn more, with nothing left over to save. You can always find reasons to spend that additional cash coming in—a new car with the latest gizmos, a stylish dress, a big sale you just can't miss—but although you are making more money, you will be making no progress.

Seventy percent of people who get a windfall (lotto winnings, inheritances, insurance payout) go broke within several years, according to research cited by the National Endowment for Financial Education.[1] How many people have said "What happened to all that money so-and-so got?" They did not know how to manage that money effectively. They started spending like there was no tomorrow. They did not know how to save.

Here's another equation to consider: Let's say you have $1,000 of income and $1,100 in bills to pay each month. Simple math: 1,000 – 1,100 = –100. That's *negative* 100. Not only do you have no money

1 "As Powerball drawing nears, former lottery winners say hitting the jackpot comes at a price," New York Daily News, accessed May 19, 2017, http://www.nydailynews.com/news/national/mega-lottery-winners-sound-advice-article-1.1209336?pgno=1.

left for anything, but you also owe somebody a hundred dollars. As that continues, you will dig yourself into a hole. What happens next month if you do not earn $1,200? That is what you must bring in so that you can pay your new round of bills and also cover what you now owe. Your $1,000 income becomes increasingly inadequate.

Many people who find themselves in that situation will borrow money. Unfortunately, they often also fail to repay it within the time they promised. God's word is clear: we are to pay what we owe. Christians need to understand that it is sinful to deal irresponsibly with debt. You can find yourself on a dark and dangerous path, full of traps.

SPENDING EXCESSES

Each of us is a consumer, which simply means we spend money to purchase things. Nothing is wrong with that, of course. It is only when you are spending in a way that prevents you from reaching your goals that you have a problem, and you must deal with it. Let's look at how and why we spend money and the financial impact of our decisions.

Overspending on clothes is a common issue. Some people rationalize how much they purchase by insisting that they must look their best for clients and colleagues. If you were to look in their closets, though, you would probably find outfits that still have the tag on them and others that have not been worn in years. The workplace should not be a fashion runway—and neither should the church sanctuary. If the cost of designer clothes is compromising your budget and your ability to save, you are doing more than just looking good. You are indulging a problem.

You can also get into trouble through impulsive buying—something catches your eye and you purchase it almost by reflex even though you really do not need it. That is a habit that can seriously hamper your ability to get on your feet financially. Many impulsive buyers, however, are unaware that they are behaving that way. They do not see their indiscriminate consumerism. Even relatively inexpensive odds and ends, tossed on the checkout counter day after day, can add up to quite a debt.

Some people are inclined to go on shopping sprees when they feel depressed or distressed about something in their lives. They are looking for something to lift their mood, but in doing so they are adding to their financial anxiety. Shopping is like a drug to them. They use it as a means of escape, and it can become an addiction not unlike substance abuse. Unless they can root out the underlying issues that are driving their behavior, they risk making a wreck of their finances.

Overspending can be a classic case of "keeping up with the Joneses." Some people, competitive by nature, set out to impress others with their financial prowess, which generally is a sign that they lack it. Few people will admit such a flaw, so take a close, honest look at yourself: Are you a gadget person? Do you rush out to acquire the latest tech toy? Somewhere inside do you feel inadequate or inferior unless you can show off a new car every few years with all the doohickeys you may never use?

Some parents cannot say no to their children. They lavish them with the latest fashionable brands so that their kids can look "fly," using up money that should be going into a college fund. Those expensive sneakers will soon be worn out and out of style. If the money is instead set aside to grow, it will buy quite a few textbooks if the kid makes it into college. As a parent, ask yourself, which is more important?

The money that you spend on such pleasures as vacationing or pursuing a hobby is well spent—provided it is not overspent. Dining out, if overdone, can cost big bucks over the weeks, months, and years. You should aim for moderation and a level of spending that always keeps your overall goals in focus. Again, consider whether this spending is preventing you from saving for retirement or from supporting your child's educational pursuits or from setting up an emergency fund to deal with life's unpredictables. When it gets in the way, it's too much.

THE CREDIT CARD TRAP

The widespread use of credit cards has worsened those spending behaviors to the point where debt is crushing numerous families. When used wisely, credit cards are a convenient tool—but it is their convenience that sets a trap for people who are inclined to abuse them. As the balance builds from month to month and the interest charges compound on a daily basis, it can be next to impossible to escape the trap.

Credit cards become an irresistible temptation for chronic overspenders to indulge their weaknesses. Easy access to easy money leads them to spend more than they have. Lacking the discipline to resist the siren song of advertisers, they slip deeper into debt.

To become the financially independent person you want to be, you must first recognize what drives your actions and behaviors. You must know what needs to change before you can do anything about it. "Where there is no vision, the people perish," we read in Proverbs 29:18. And in Hosea 4:6: "My people are destroyed for lack of knowledge." We must not remain in darkness. Once we understand a problem and bring it to light, we are finally on our way to the solution.

THE BOTTOM LINE

If you are to be financially independent, you must not carry excessive debt or you will be unable to save and invest. Too much debt generally is the result of chronic overspending and failure to live within one's means.

CHAPTER 4

FIGHTING THE SPENDING HABIT

Put on the whole armor of God that ye may be able to stand against the wiles of the devil.

—Ephesians 6:11

In his letter to the Ephesians, Paul said we must put on the armor of God to fend off the powers and principalities that would lead us astray. That line from Scripture is the war cry of the saints.

Prepare to go to war, now, against the powers that are trying to pull you down financially. They come from both within and without, beckoning you to spend far beyond your means on things you do not need and maybe did not even know you wanted. Overspending causes more financial struggles than lack of income, but either way, you still need to get started on a savings plan, however modest.

Product marketers do their best to persuade us to pull out our wallets. Advertising bombards us. The marketers have long known that sex sells, and so we, and our children, are surrounded with come-hither images in various stages of undress. They are selling happiness, as well: *Buy this, and you'll be filled with joy!* Though we may know the real source of peace does not lie in material things, those persistent messages suggest we can spend our way to a better life. They try to offer a shortcut to happiness.

It can be hard to resist. So many people yearn to feel attractive and to fill an emptiness inside. This is where we need the whole armor of God to do battle against the wiles of the devil and of the flesh. The marketers target our sinful nature to tempt us to buy their products and services with the money that we should be saving and investing for far better purposes. God's word tells us that we are battling "spiritual wickedness in high places," and often that wickedness enters our homes and hearts via our television sets and Internet connections. We must resist those messages if we are to be mighty men and women of wealth.

THE POWER OF CONTENTMENT

In the previous chapter, we looked at some of the reasons that people overspend. We need to overcome the worldly attitudes that keep us in financial bondage. Rather than constantly searching for that shortcut to happiness, we need to understand the meaning of true contentment.

To be content is to be happy enough with what you have or with your situation and circumstances. Paul also had this to say in his letter to the Philippians: "For I have learned, in whatsoever state I am, therewith to be content."

If that seems to contradict the message that we should put on the armor of God to fight the dark powers, consider why it is important to be content. It empowers you. When you are content, you are better able to avoid and resist the urges and obstacles and temptations that come your way. You are therefore in a better position to advance financially to the next level.

Let's look at some examples of life situations that illustrate the power of contentment.

- Those sexy boots that were marked $500 are now half off. If you are content with what you have, you can resist the urge to buy them. Boots wear out if you use them; more likely they would gather dust in your closet. Money, however, has the potential to grow—and now you have the use of that $250 that otherwise would have vanished. Why not invest it in something better that would benefit you and your family down the road?
- You see an advertisement for that fully loaded car you have been wanting—and it has a year-end discount of 50 percent, with zero percent financing for three years. Nothing is wrong with the car you've been driving, but what a deal! If you are content, you can fight off the urge to buy. You can say, "Oh, forget that, I need to stick to my financial goals first." By recognizing and accepting your financial situation for what it is, you will not fall victim to the excesses of discontent. You will stay on track. I met a young man, a recent graduate, who invested in property when his friends were buying expensive cars. He was content with a car that cost him $5,000 rather than $100,000. Guess who will be far ahead of his peers in a few decades, when those expensive cars are rusting in a scrapyard.
- Your daughter or son asks for a $500 winter coat, a $200 designer belt, or some expensive footwear. Some parents

would agree, believing the purchase to be an expression of love. But what if such an expense is not in your budget? This is an opportunity to teach your children about contentment. They need to see through your example that they cannot get everything they want and that they can be happy nonetheless. You can explain that if they accept what they have now, you will be better able to help them financially at a more critical time. Is that not a greater expression of love?

- A couple at your church suggests that you dine out together, but you know that the bill would blow your monthly allowance. Many people would accept the invitation anyway, and they might even pick up the whole tab trying to impress—as if it is possible to buy friendship. But if you are content, you will feel comfortable in declining. You might even tell the couple that you and your spouse are cutting back to save for a bigger goal. By accepting your current situation, you are keeping the door open to something better. When you spend beyond your means, you are slamming that door shut.

Such is the power of being content. You accept your current state knowing that you are empowering yourself and your family for a better tomorrow. And through your example, you could inspire others to examine their finances and make the changes that will benefit them in the future. Many people get into financial difficulties. You can be the light to help guide them out.

"I waited patiently for the Lord," we read in Psalm 40:1. That tells us that contentment is an active state. To be patient as you wait means that you have made a conscious decision to stay calm. It requires a force of will. You must focus on restraint and relaxation. That helps you to be alert and attentive to the opportunities around you.

Many Christians, however, cite that verse to justify a passive and defeatist way of thinking and living. Whatever their religion or background, people commonly present themselves as powerless. I, too, once fell into the habit of saying, "I'm stuck." My wife and my son both challenged me one day about why I would say that. It turned out, as I examined my motives, that I was looking for an excuse to spend. Sometimes, by ruling out other options and possibilities, we tell ourselves that we might as well buy this or that. We can pretend it is our only choice—and that is what I was doing.

If you are in that situation, a better attitude would be to tell yourself that your only choice is to *not* buy something. Once you develop an overspending habit, it can be difficult to stop. Do not think that you are powerless, however. Do not accept that you must live paycheck to paycheck and never get out of your rut. With the power of contentment, you will be able to turn away from the temptations that distract you from reaching your financial goals.

You will face a host of challenges on your path to financial independence. To succeed, you will need to come to grips with who you are. You must confront your attitudes about money. If you are a parent, it is high time that you do so. Bad habits that are learned young tend to persist and can hinder your children later in life. Unless you teach them about money and show them a better way, you could see them repeat your mistakes. That is not the legacy you want to leave.

THE BOTTOM LINE

By learning to be content with what you have, you can resist the temptation to spend more and more to acquire stuff you don't need. To be content is to actively decide to live more simply while keeping alert to all opportunities.

CHAPTER 5

BUILDING THE FOUNDATION

He is like a man who built a house, and dug deep, and laid the foundation on a rock.

—Luke 6:48

For years, even as my financial awareness grew, I still struggled. Though I had learned much, I held on to some spending habits that were not preparing me financially. I had not confronted the problem or even thought about it. I did not look inward to challenge and change my behaviors. When the storm came and the torrent beat upon my financial house, it collapsed. It was not built on rock. It lacked a deep, solid foundation.

To grow in grace on your Christian walk, you know that you must develop a new way of thinking and behaving. Likewise, you need a new way of thinking and behaving as you grow in financial awareness. You need to think of money differently, with a deeper knowledge of finances, and then find practical applications in your life.

"Behavioral finance" is a relatively new field of research that examines how people's attitudes toward money influence their financial decision making. For a great many people, money management is not an objective, rational activity. Research has shown that even financial professionals can be led astray by emotions of the moment that often are rooted in the past.

Those emotions are the internal barriers that can get in the way of your financial independence. That is why I have been emphasizing that becoming aware of those thoughts, feelings, and behaviors and confronting them is an essential early step toward making the necessary changes. I once accepted the lie, for example, that you need a lot of money to start a savings or investing program. Had I started earlier, how much more would I have today to help others?

SOWING IN RICH SOIL

In Matthew 13, Jesus told the parable of the sower of seeds. Some of those seeds fell by the wayside, where the birds devoured them. Some fell on stony ground, where the sun scorched the seedlings and they withered for lack of root. Some fell among thorns that choked the growth. And some fell on fertile soil and brought forth a bountiful crop.

"Who hath ears to hear, let him hear," Christ concluded. Are you open to the lesson here? To become a mighty person of wealth, you need to plant in the right soil. Your financial harvest will depend on whether you can recognize what will stunt or destroy your growth. What will scorch and choke your crop, and what will devour the seeds before they can sprout?

If you have ears to hear, then you have the tools to become aware. Jesus was telling us to listen up. Do not overlook the truths as they are presented to you. Examine yourself and those around you. Carefully assess your financial circumstances, and sow wisely.

Some people gather plenty of information and advice but do nothing with it. They toss it by the wayside, and it never grows. They experience no internal change in how they think and feel about money. They exhibit no outward change in their actions or behaviors. They stay in financial bondage.

Others will cut back on their spending for a month or two, put a few dollars in the bank, or pay off some of their debt—but soon revert to their old ways. They proclaim again that they feel stuck and have no choice in their spending. They feel discontented with the cutbacks that have allowed them to start getting ahead. These are the people who have planted on stony soil. Their efforts wither. They cease to grow.

Saddest of all, to me, are the ones who sow their seeds among thorns. Though the soil is rich and deep, perfect for a good harvest, the thorns also like it and take over. For these people, the pressures of life become too much. As they take off on their financial journey, they must face a variety of financial demands. Their children and other loved ones may not understand this newfound caution about spending. Those who once came to them for handouts now regard them as miserly. It's so easy to give in and let those thorns have their way, choking off the growth.

Let the seeds you sow take root on good ground. Take the time to absorb financial truths, and apply them daily. Establish a budget and stick with it. Pay down your debt. Build up your savings and investments. Those seeds soon will sprout, and as you tend to the new growth, you eventually can reap a fruitful harvest. You will gain financial peace of mind. One day you will be able to retire on your own terms and timing.

On what kind of soil are you planting? To answer that question, look within and look without. What is getting in your way? If you have been letting wise teachings go in one ear and out the other, ask yourself why. If you are reading this book, you are demonstrating that you want to learn. So know this: you do have a choice. You can choose to plant on fertile ground, where you can cultivate and protect the crop as it grows and matures through the seasons. Be the good gardener.

KEEPING YOUR FOCUS

God's word is clear: we are to think about what we are doing and why we are doing it. We are expected to keep on doing what's right. Let's look at some ways to build a foundation of financial responsibility, starting with some sound advice about fundamentals:

- Keep track of your major annual expenses. For example, if you know that your car insurance bill will be $2,400 for the year, you should be budgeting $200 a month toward that expense. Do not spend that money. It must be available when the time comes to pay.
- Put the credit cards away. Take them out of your wallet and tuck them into the back of a drawer or wherever they will be safe but out of the way. A lot of spending is impulsive. If your credit card is not available, you cannot use it. You do not want to climb out of debt just to fall right back into it.
- Budget your discretionary money. For example, perhaps you are able to give yourself $300 a month to spend however you like. You can manage that money in a number of ways. You might keep it in cash for use as needed, or you might load that money onto a prepaid debit card. Just know that

once that money is gone, it is gone. Don't go digging in that drawer for your credit cards.

- Buy everything with cash. Those plastic credit cards might not feel like real money. Debit cards can get you in trouble, too, particularly when they are tied to an account that you use to pay bills. A cash-only system can help you keep track of how much you are actually spending. You get a different feeling when you are counting out those greenbacks from your wallet. It feels real when you see how many $20 bills you are shelling out for a belt buckle. It can be hard to live by cash in this age of plastic, but you should do what you must to stay on track. It's like dieting. I try to keep away from what will tempt me to overindulge. That's why I don't keep doughnuts in my house.

Along your path to financial responsibility, be prepared for changes in your relationships. If people have been looking to you for handouts, they may wonder what's up with you. They may whisper that you seem less generous. What you are being is more responsible. When you are ready, and when it is appropriate, you should tell the important people in your life that you are cutting back to get your financial house in order. Let them know that this will be the new you and why.

"Neither do men light a candle and put it under a bushel, but on a candlestick; and it giveth light unto all that are in the house," Jesus said in Matthew 5:15. As others observe that you are walking on the path of financial empowerment, they will feel inspired to get their own financial houses in order. In that way, you can be a blessing and a help to them. They will seek out your advice and suggestions. You can become a financial light for those who dwell in the darkness of debt and despair. Your testimony will help them to see that they can overcome, too.

Nonetheless, some may try to sabotage your efforts. Those closest to you could become your biggest threat to financial independence, even if they do not recognize what they do. Friends and family may pressure you to spend money on things that you do not need, making a mess of your budget. As their own finances spiral out of control, they may look to you for help. You will need the resolve to stand firmly on your path, as Jesus did when Peter tried to persuade him not to do what he was destined to do.

DIGGING DEEP

If your foundation is deep, you will be prepared to weather the storms along the way. As you begin to build your financial house, dig deep to lay that foundation firmly on rock so that nothing can shake it. Dig below the shifting sand of your attitudes, thoughts, and feelings about money. Unless you shovel those aside, you will leave your house vulnerable.

Be patient. It's like losing weight. You shed a few pounds and nobody notices, perhaps not even you. As you keep at it every day, though, the results in time become clear to all. That's when you truly come to appreciate your dieting diligence.

It's when the storms of life are raging around you that you will be glad you were diligent about digging deep before building your financial house. When the sun breaks out again, you will emerge safe and strong, with your walls still standing. That's when you will know that all that foundational work was worth it. You got to the bottom of it all. While others will see their house collapse around them. You stayed on track and focused during those rough times in your life.

THE BOTTOM LINE

You need to build a strong financial foundation to withstand the storms of life. Dig deep to uncover the unshakeable truth, and examine the validity of your own understandings and attitudes. Keep your focus when others seem to be discouraging you.

CHAPTER 6

CONFRONTING YOUR FINANCIAL SITUATION

The Lord is the strength of my life: of whom shall I be afraid?

—Psalm 27:1

When things are not going well in life, people often try to avoid them—and that includes their financial problems. Who wants to confront a mess? If you do not deal with those issues, however, they worsen.

It is time, therefore, to roll up your sleeves and get your hands dirty and start taking control of your financial life.

First things first: List all your debts, including the $25 that you owe Aunt Jean. List how much you owe to whom and the interest rate, if any, like this:

OWED TO	AMOUNT	INTEREST ON DEBT
Aunt Jean	$25	0
Credit card 1	$800	12%
Credit card 2	$1,300	18%
Store card	$2,725	24%
Car note	$9,000	6%
IRS	$4,500	Who knows?

Next, review your credit card spending over the last six months. That will help you to see the pattern of your buying and spending habits. By analyzing what is going on with your money, you can clarify your financial situation.

Consider whether most of your credit card spending is truly for necessities. If that is the case, you might have an income problem. Your issue may be how much money is coming in and not so much how it is going out. We will look at that problem, too, but first examine your credit card statements: Do you have expenses that you could avoid?

For example, do you buy a lot of things for the children, grandchildren, or other relatives and friends? If so, ask yourself why. Why are you going into debt for that reason? Some just feel that it is their obligation. Some feel responsible for a past wrong. You will no doubt have your reasons, but you need to think them through and come to grips with your motivations if you are to change your behaviors. Figure out what has led you down this road that is veering away from your financial independence.

You may very well discover that you have a spending problem. A friend recently told me she found a rack of clothes in her closet with the tags still on them. She had purchased them a year earlier and never worn them. If you have had such an experience—and there are many things besides clothes that you may be buying unnecessarily—consider it a hint that you need to make some changes. Ask yourself why you felt those purchases were so important that they were worth going into debt. Once you understand your overspending habit, you will be better able to kick it.

When you have finished your complete list of creditors, congratulate yourself. You are now actively taking charge of your financial life. You can be proud that you have taken a great first step. Many people never get even that far.

IS BANKRUPTCY A SOLUTION?

If you find that your debt is truly out of control, let's deal with the most difficult and emotional situation first. As you look at your total debt, do you find yourself saying that there is no way you can pay this back? Seeing everything you owe listed together, do you feel overwhelmed?

If that is the case, you need professional assistance as soon as possible from a trusted advisor who can clearly explain your options to you. There are a variety of strategies for dealing with that effectively, but if you feel that you are in an impossible situation, you may be considering bankruptcy. Because that is the roughest and toughest decision that you might need to make, let's examine that option first and get it out of the way.

Going through bankruptcy is stressful. You must not take it lightly or pursue it without considering all the alternatives. Be aware that your credit report will reflect the bankruptcy filing for several years. It will be visible to potential landlords if you wish to rent an apartment, and lenders will see it if you wish to buy a car or make other purchases on credit. You can think of bankruptcy as an opportunity for a fresh start, but if you are not careful you can dig yourself into the same situation again. In any case, you will go through a period in which you will need to repair your credit reputation.

After declaring bankruptcy, you should be working with a trusted advisor to get your finances fully on track and reestablish a reliable track record. I help people with strategies to rebuild their credit as quickly as possible, even right after a bankruptcy filing, and we also work on underlying attitudes about spending and saving to make sure they stay out of the pit. Credit card lenders will sometimes target people within months after their debts have been cleared in bankruptcy, luring them back into trouble with ultra-high interest rates. They have a fresh start, yet they fall back into the old pattern.

How might you know that you are a candidate for bankruptcy? You might feel afraid to answer the phone because it could be a creditor calling. Your voicemail might be full. You might try to avoid running into the deacon of your church because you owe him $200. In fact, you might stop going to church because you owe money to so many people there. You might have a pile of notices for bills thirty days or sixty days past due. Your bank accounts might have been placed on hold. If any part of this sounds like your situation, consider bankruptcy.

There are two types of bankruptcy. For both, you will need professional assistance with the rules and regulations involved. You can get help from a number of nonprofit budget and credit services, or you may have an Employee Assistance Program (EAP) through your employer that you can contact for support and guidance. You can also learn more from a variety of books, blogs, and agencies, both profit and nonprofit. The process is complex, and we cannot cover it all here.

One type of bankruptcy is called Chapter 13, in which you basically are reorganizing your debts without debt forgiveness. The other type, and the more common one, is called Chapter 7, in which you are asking the courts to discharge your debts and give you a clean slate and a fresh start.

Chapter 7 bankruptcy does not clear every debt. You will not be forgiven any back child support payments, for example. Student loans can be discharged, but that very seldom happens. If you owe money to the IRS, you may have some options; you should speak with a tax expert about that.

Do not wait too long before filing for bankruptcy. It is a myth that a lot of people eagerly run to declare bankruptcy as soon as they can. Bankruptcy amounts to an acknowledgment that your financial life has spiraled out of control. You are asking for an intervention to straighten yourself out. Not many people want to declare such things. Add to that the emotional stress they are under, and they often wind up waiting too long.

Don't let that be you. If you think bankruptcy may be an option, talk to a professional right away. You need guidance both in deciding whether this is an appropriate route for you and in navigating the process if you go ahead with it. The longer you wait, the longer it will take you to recover. If you truly need a fresh start, the law provides this relief. If you and your advisor determine that it is appropriate for you, file soon. Time is of the essence.

Declaring bankruptcy does not mean that your troubles are over. You need to deal with whatever got you into that situation or you could find yourself back in the same mess.

REPAYMENT STRATEGIES

Short of bankruptcy, you can choose from a variety of strategies to find the one that works best for you—and that will be a choice that not only lowers your debt but enables you to keep out of it. It will take time, but do not be discouraged. If you stop, you will no longer be on the road to financial independence.

Let's look at that list again:

OWED TO	AMOUNT	INTEREST ON DEBT
Aunt Jean	$25	0
Credit card 1	$800	12%
Credit card 2	$1,300	18%
Store card	$2,725	24%
Car note	$9,000	6%
IRS	$4,500	Who knows?

Which of those debts would you deal with first? The smart money would say to pay off the store card. That only makes sense: It carries the highest interest rate, meaning that more of each payment you make goes to the issuer of the card and less goes toward what you owe. Therefore, the standard reasoning is that you should get rid of that debt first because it is the biggest drain on your money. Based on that principle, you should pay down your debts in this order: the store card, credit card 2, credit card 1, the IRS, the car note, and finally Aunt Jean.

Paying the debts in that prescribed order, however, may not be what is best for you. Let's say that it would take you three months to pay off the store card but that you would be able to pay all of what you owe on credit card 1 in one month. That card, however, is accruing interest at only half the rate of the store card, so some would say it makes no sense to pay it off first. But how do you feel? Would you find it gratifying to knock that smaller debt off your list? Would that make you feel that you are truly getting your financial house in order? Would it encourage you to stay on this new path to financial freedom? If so, then that is what you should do. What is best for you is the course of action most likely to keep you on track. What is best for you is what empowers you.

Perhaps you will decide that paying off the IRS debt first is best for you. You find it highly stressful to get those letters from the government, and you want the IRS to get off your case. You feel that would encourage you to stick with your debt management plan. Do it that way then. The best plan is the one that you finish.

Or maybe the best debt to pay first is the $25 that you owe sweet Aunt Jean, even though she is not charging you a cent of interest and is not going to be sending you reminders. By keeping your promise to pay her back promptly, you will be demonstrating to her, and to all your family, that you are determined to be responsible. It is a small amount, but you get back a big dividend in goodwill. As you can see, what is best for you may not be what some analyst with a calculator would dictate. Yes, they are generally right but not always about what is right for you.

You might have enough savings in the bank to pay off some or all of your debts. Let's say you have $3,000, and it is earning just pennies a month in interest. You would be better off using some of that money to pay down your high-interest credit cards.

Look for ways that you might be able to pay your debts at lower interest and under more favorable terms. Consider calling the credit card companies to ask them to lower their rates. The worst that could happen is they will say no. A consolidation loan is another strategy that can help you pay off your debt more efficiently. If you are eligible, a lender may roll your other debts into one loan at a lower rate so that you will have just one monthly payment that can be significantly less than the others combined. The strategies can get tricky, so work with a professional to identify the advantages, disadvantages, and potential traps. As a comprehensive financial planner, I assist my clients with their entire financial picture, which includes finding the most efficient ways to handle their debts.

A second mortgage, or home equity loan, might be beneficial if that is an option for you. You would use this new loan to pay off your other debts. Your new terms would allow you to pay what you owe sooner and more efficiently, at a much lower interest rate. Considerably more of each payment would go toward paying down your debt instead of lining the lenders' pockets. In addition, the interest that you pay on the second mortgage might be tax deductible—a benefit that you do not get with your other loans.

You should understand, however, that this is no longer an unsecured loan. Your debt is now tied to the value of your home, and you will be putting your home on the line. If you are unable to pay back what you owe, you could lose it. You should avoid using your home as if it were an ATM, expecting it to cover your growing debts while you do nothing to address the underlying attitudes that are getting you into trouble.

CHECKING YOUR CREDIT HISTORY

As you are striving to reduce your debt, you need to monitor your credit records. Your credit history will significantly influence the terms of your loans and other obligations. If your score is not up to par, for example, you could face higher premiums on your auto, homeowners, and life insurance policies. In some states, an employer might be allowed to pull your credit report when deciding whether to hire you, although the information provided is limited. It is particularly important that your credit remain in good standing if you work in certain careers, such as in the financial sector or in sensitive positions with the military. I have seen cases where people were denied promotions and were required to work with a professional on a strategy for debt and financial management.

Another reason to regularly review your credit report is that you might find mistakes in it. The credit bureaus—there are three, Experian, Equifax, and Transunion—sometimes mix up similar names. And sometimes they report negative information incorrectly: you might see the same delinquency listed three times, for instance, or a debt that you have paid off that still appears to be in collections. You could even discover that you have been the victim of identity theft, another big reason to keep a close watch.

The three monitoring agencies may each report details of your credit record differently. That is why it is important to review all three to make sure that they have included favorable items and are not including unfavorable ones by error. Do not wait until you need credit before conducting this review. You want to get any problems out of the way well in advance.

You can obtain those credit reports once a year from www.annualcreditreport.com, which the government has set up to provide people with free access. I do help people obtain those reports as needed. Sometimes people can be to overwhelmed to get a handle on what is going on. You should take advantage of this opportunity, reviewing each of the three reports, one at a time.

Order your report first from Experian, then Equifax, and then Transunion. Start by reviewing the Experian report line by line. If you find an error, you can file a dispute. If it is resolved in your favor, you are entitled to another free report. After you have resolved every issue and are satisfied with the updated report, then move on to order the report from the next agency. This can be a slow, involved process, along with being stressful, but it is worth your time.

As you do your reviews with all three bureaus, make sure you recognize each of the credit accounts that they list. If you do not, call the company for further information. You may find out that you had just forgotten about it. If you see that something has damaged your credit, make sure it is legitimate. If it is not, take the time to challenge it. It can be a difficult task, particularly if you have a number of issues to confront, but do not ignore it. I once spent a long time on the phone resolving an erroneous report claiming that a medical bill went unpaid. Remember that you do not have to get everything done in a week. Do a little at a time, slowly and steadily, to get the job done.

THE BOTTOM LINE

You need to be proactive in dealing with your debts, deciding which to pay first and the most efficient way to do so. Take care to monitor your credit report regularly. If you must consider bankruptcy, do so with great caution and professional guidance.

CHAPTER 7

INCOME AND SPENDING

For which of you, intending to build a tower, sitteth not down first, and counteth the cost, whether he have sufficient to finish it?

—Luke 14:28

Now it is time to examine your monthly expenses and your monthly income. In doing so, you will be looking to streamline your spending so that you can further pay down your debts, as we discussed in the last chapter, while building a savings and investing account for your future.

First, establish how much money is coming in. Gather a month's worth of your paychecks and write down the net amount that you receive after withholdings. If you get regular income from any other source, such as alimony, write that down, too, and total the amounts.

How much of that total should you be committing toward your savings and paying down your debt? Some people just come up with some figure that seems to fit—say, $300 a month—and try to adjust their spending habits to make sure it is available. But there are pitfalls to that approach. It may be more than you are able to set aside, or perhaps you could devote a greater amount each month, thereby building your savings or reducing your debt more quickly. Either way, you could end up feeling discouraged and tempted to forget the whole thing.

I encourage you to come up with a monthly plan so that you know just where you stand and how much you can do. Follow that biblical advice to count the cost.

MAKING THE HARD DECISIONS

Start by tallying your monthly expenses, and be honest with yourself. If you know you spend five dollars a day on coffee, include that. And don't forget those new outfits you buy several times a year for special church services. Include that cost, too. Be sure to include expenses that you pay only once a year, such as your auto insurance premium; divide by twelve to get the monthly amount. Here is how your list might look:

EXPENSE	MONTHLY AMOUNT
Cable	$200
Rent	$1,200
Light	$125
Car insurance	$200 ($2,400/12)
Car upkeep	$90 ($1,080/12)
Lunch and coffee	$300 ($15 × 20)
Credit card debt	$600
Cell phone	$150
Food shopping	$400
Miscellaneous	$525

This is where you must make some hard decisions. If you are to become a mighty person of wealth, like Boaz, it is time to take control of your spending habits and patterns. As you look at that list, where could you save?

What I see right away is that you are paying nearly as much each month for lunches and coffee as for your food shopping. It is much cheaper, of course, to prepare a meal at home than to buy it in a restaurant. If you packed a lunch just half the time, you could save $150 a month. And look at that cable bill. Why not try going without cable for a few months to see if it really matters that much to you? Or buy a cheaper package. Ouch, you say? Just remember that controlling your spending is the key to economic freedom.

Saving is like dieting. Some are committed to losing weight and succeed, and some, for various reasons, try but still struggle. I confess that I am among the latter. When it comes to wealth creation, however, I have learned that there is no secret formula. What works is this: you must be determined to keep your commitment to control spending.

Wealthy people can lose it all unless they effectively manage their spending. We often hear of rich and famous people who have had big money troubles. Just a few examples: the rapper 50 Cent, football player Michael Vick, singer Toni Braxton, commentator Larry King, and singer Dionne Warwick. All have gone to bankruptcy court. You can make $1 million a year, but if you spend $2 million a year you will still go broke—you will just go broke in style.

It takes strength to overcome this problem. "Endure hardness," the apostle Paul advised Timothy, urging him to be watchful in all things. This is hardness. Controlling spending, for most people, is hard work. Our culture aims to separate us from our money—even from the money we have not yet earned. That is why you need to understand what motivates you and why you may be struggling with your spending. Your thoughts and feelings are the greatest hindrance to financial independence.

Paul understood his own struggle to avoid doing wrong, even when he knew full well what was right. We know what we should do, but it is still a battle. You must fight to bring your spending into line for a greater and higher purpose. Whether you are a saint or a sinner, you need to gain that control. There is no magic pill that will cure your finances, any more than there is one that will make you lose weight. It takes discipline, consistency, and hard work.

IDENTIFYING WHERE TO CUT BACK

So let's get to work and identify more ways to manage your spending. You will need to honestly assess where in your budget you can scale back. What can you and your family do without? If you are like many parents, for example, you spend a lot of money on your children. But is it really serving them well, or might it be more of a disservice? Where else can you make sacrifices, even to save a little here and there? Those dollars add up.

As you manage your spending, you will need the discipline to stay within the budget that you establish. Certain expenses will be necessities. You must pay for them, no matter what, such as the rent or mortgage, the electric bill, your phone fees, and transportation. Other expenses will be discretionary. You choose to spend money on these nonessentials. Again I think of the example of buying lunch. While training to be a firefighter, my nephew Jamel and his fellow cadets had to pack sandwiches every day. The training facility had no cafeteria, not even a microwave or toaster oven. Why not follow their example even if you do have the discretion to purchase your meals?

For many of your expenses, you have the power of choice—and you can choose to use it wisely. Once you acknowledge that you have that power in your hands, you can put it to good use: you can make those hard decisions on where you can cut back and how much of that money you will allocate toward savings and how much toward paying down your debt each month.

COUNT THE CONSEQUENCES

The sooner the better. Overspending has consequences. I know—I once made poor life choices and had to deal with the resulting hardships. No one had told me about the importance of saving and investing. I am grateful that you are reading this book so that you might avoid such troubles. Let me tell you a fact of life: sooner or later, you must pay for your indulgences. "For they have sown the wind," we read in Hosea 8:7, "and they shall reap the whirlwind."

A few decades from now, you do not want to regret, as you continue to struggle financially, how you wasted a lot of money—if you can even remember where it went. In hindsight, you will wonder why you thought it was so important to spend your money that way, but then it will be too late. You will not be able to travel back in time to undo what you did or to do what you should have done.

You know the parable of the prodigal son in Luke 15. We rejoice as the father welcomes home the young man, worn out from riotous living. We focus on the celebration and merriment. He who was lost has been found; he who was dead is alive. We feel happy knowing that we can be redeemed after a dreadful mistake. And that is wonderful.

However, a critical part of that parable, and one seldom discussed, is what the father says to his other son, who had stayed, invested his time and sweat, and labored with his father to build the business: "Son, thou art ever with me, and all that I have is thine." Yes, the younger son has been restored and is back with the family, but he is left with nothing. Yes, the Lord is generous and merciful, but he holds us responsible for our actions. The younger son will forever be dependent on his older brother's generosity.

Count the consequences. If you put your financial life at risk and waste all your money, how can you expect to support your children, your grandchildren, and the church ministry? Your life actions will bear fruit, and that fruit may be sweet and juicy or it may be sour and bitter. What you are doing right now will make the difference. I am not exaggerating or trying to scare you. I am telling it to you straight.

I understand that cutting back on your spending can feel oppressive, particularly when your finances are way out of balance and you need to sacrifice a lot to set things right. Many people who have racked up major debt do not want to dial back their lifestyle to pay for the problems of the past. Do not let that be you. Now is the time to find your financial balance and keep it that way.

THE BOTTOM LINE

To attain financial success, develop the essential disciplines of keeping your income and expenses in balance and budgeting carefully so that you have money to pay off debt and save toward your future.

CHAPTER 8

MANAGING YOUR TAXES

Render therefore unto Caesar the things which are Caesar's, and unto God the things that are God's.

—Matthew 22:21

Let's say that April 15 comes around and you find yourself in debt to the IRS. It happens to many people. Whether it's a few hundred dollars or a few thousand dollars, it represents poor planning, particularly if you will be struggling to write that check. Your shortfall in meeting your tax obligation amounts to a loan from the IRS. The amount that you have "borrowed" may come as a surprise—in which case, it is unlikely that you have budgeted a penny toward paying it back.

Consider your choices now: To fit this tax bill into your budget, you will need to take out something else. Where will you curtail your spending? Is there some other bill that you intend to skip, or will you contribute less to your savings account? Perhaps you will take the high road and find the money by rearranging your vacation plans or postponing something else you wanted to do or buy.

Let's look first at the biblical teaching on taxes. When the Pharisees sought to discredit Jesus, they asked him whether the imperial Roman tax was legal. They reasoned that if he said yes, he would be condemned by most of the Jewish population, which despised the tax, and that if he said no, he would be in serious trouble with the Roman authorities. In his reply, Christ pointed out that it was Caesar's image on the Roman coin, and therefore those who were subject to the tax should give back to Caesar the things that were his—and to God the things that were God's. Jesus was affirming the moral responsibility to pay taxes, while emphasizing that we are to give the ultimate tribute to God for what matters most.

That does not mean that when rendering unto Caesar, we need to pay more than necessary. In this chapter, we will look at ways that you can legitimately reduce your tax bill. The federal tax code, thousands of pages long, is filled with incentives and breaks, and the intention is not to make rich people richer. They exist because the government wants to promote certain things such as homeownership and charitable giving. However, many people, of all income levels, are not aware of them and pass up the opportunity for significant tax savings.

As a tax professional, I have often seen situations in which people have not taken advantage of provisions and strategies available to them in the tax code. I recently talked with a couple who could have saved $60,000 in taxes over a two-year period if they had simply invested in good advice. In preparing returns over the years, I have seen thousands of people's tax situations. I have seen their mistakes, and I know what works and what does not work. I know that working with someone knowledgeable about the code can produce savings far greater than the fee for the service.

For example, one tax break in the IRS code allows you to deduct what you pay to a knowledgeable professional for preparing your return. In other words, the government will help you to hire a tax expert to look for every possible way to assure that you are not paying more than your fair share. That is an awesome benefit.

One of my clients recently saved $7,000 by working with me to determine the best strategy for next year's tax preparations. He seized the opportunity to talk to a professional who could explain how the tax code could be better used to his advantage with some early planning.

I am not putting down the do-it-yourself types who want to prepare their own returns. Some people are very good at it. They do their homework and research, and when I have reviewed their returns I have perhaps pointed out one small error to save them money and then sent them on their way. If you decide to prepare your own return, just be aware of what you are getting into. You should have a broad knowledge of the tax code and the time and resources to do it right.

TAX-SAVING OPPORTUNITIES

Following are some examples of where people might be able to save more in taxes. If you believe that a tax provision applies to you, consult with a professional to make sure that is the case. Everyone's situation will be different.

Claiming a child as a dependent

Don't think that just because your child is working that you cannot claim him or her as a dependent on your return. I have had clients who were supporting an eighteen-year-old child still living at home but believed they were not eligible for that deduction. There might be other reasons that they would be correct, but the child's working status is not necessarily one of them.

The earned income tax credit

This is a refundable credit available to low- and moderate-income working individuals and couples, particularly those with children. However, the IRS estimates that 20 percent of tax filers who are eligible for the EIC do not claim it. I recently had to point out to a couple that they were eligible for the EIC even though they were claiming their eighteen-year-old as a dependent.

Pretax savings

The IRS has made provisions for setting aside money before it is taxed when that money is designated for certain uses. It usually will be in your best financial interest to take advantage of those opportunities. Let's look at a few examples.

Transportation pretax savings. If you take public transportation, you can save on taxes. Let's say you earn $30,000 a year and pay $200 a month to commute by bus or train. That's $2,400 annually. You could get some of that money back into your pocket. To see how that works, consider what you would pay if you did not take advantage of the pretax savings. Your entire $30,000 gross income would be taxed at 20 percent, leaving you $24,000 net. After paying for transportation, you would have $21,600 left. With the pretax savings program, however, your transportation expenses would be deducted from each paycheck, reducing the amount subject to tax. Your taxable income for the year therefore would be $27,600, not $30,000. That means the 20 percent income tax would only amount to $5,520, not $6,000. In other words, you would have $22,080 left, not $21,600. Your annual savings: $480. Your commuting expense has not changed, but your tax expense has gone down significantly.

WITHOUT PRETAX SAVINGS	WITH PRETAX SAVINGS
$30,000 gross income	$30,000 gross income
–$6,000 20% tax	–$2,400 transportation
$24,000	$27,600
–$2,400 transportation	–$5,520 20% tax
$21,600 for you	$22,080 for you
	$480 extra saved

Over time, those tax savings add up to a lot of potential. Even if your annual savings stayed at $480, in fifteen years you would have $7,200—and all you had to do was claim what was yours under that tax provision. I'm sure you can think of a lot of good uses for that money, including paying down debt or investing it wisely so that it grows to an even greater amount. And because you have lowered your gross income, you could be eligible for more EIC benefits. That is the power of the tax code when used strategically.

Medical bills. If your company offers a flexible spending account, you can put some of your money into it for tax savings. This is a use-it-or-lose-it account, but you can still safely take advantage of it. Figure how much you spend each year on medical expenses—doctor visits, co-pays, medications, eyeglasses, and even medical transportation. Let's say it's about $500 a year. You can confidently put $200 into the account without fear of overfunding it. You reduce your taxable income by that amount, which gives you a $40 tax savings. Over fifteen years, you save $600 without any sacrifice.

Maximizing your deductions

Some people avoid the "long form" because they are afraid of an audit—but the IRS audits people who file the short form as well. If you have all your documentation, take the deductions to which you are entitled. It may turn out that the short form is to your advantage, but you need to find out for sure. Let's look at some examples of what you can deduct.

- You can deduct your tithes and offerings to the church. Pay by check to document what you have given. The church, which must be recognized as a charity, can also send you a letter documenting your giving.
- You can deduct clothing and household goods and other items that you donate to organizations that are recognized as a charity. They will provide you with documentation of your donation.

- If you are currently looking for work, whether you are employed or unemployed, you can deduct your job search expenses, including professional resume services, the cost of transportation to your interviews, and even the expense of buying and mailing thank-you notes.
- You can deduct what you paid a professional to prepare the previous year's tax return. If you purchased a book or software to help you, you can deduct that cost as well.
- If you had to move more than fifty miles to get closer to your job, you can deduct the moving expense. You do not even need to itemize to claim that deduction.
- You can deduct the amount you paid in student loan interest.

This list goes on and on. You must abide by the rules and regulations, of course, and everyone's situation is different. Always check to make sure you are qualified.

Savings for the self-employed

If you are self-employed, the deductions you can take will depend on your industry and the nature of your expenses. The deductions might include transportation, business meals, cell phone, professional services, and so on.

I strongly recommend working with a tax professional to identify your savings and planning strategies. And remember, that service fee is deductible as well. As a tax professional myself, I have helped many people save significantly. Some are at a level where they do not need my services, and I tell them so. They have taken the time to thoroughly educate themselves about taxes. Most, however, need good guidance.

Only you know how much you know. I'm here to help as needed. And remember that your tax situation is only part of your financial picture. You need to look beyond a single year. Your tax strategy needs to fit into your larger vision and long-range objectives.

THE BOTTOM LINE

The federal tax code is filled with opportunities to save, but you cannot take advantage of them unless you are aware of them. A professional can help you to keep your tax obligation to a minimum.

CHAPTER 9

SETTING YOUR GOALS

I have fought a good fight, I have finished my course, I have kept the faith.

—2 Timothy 4:7

On his Christian journey, Paul stayed true to what he believed all the way to the end, despite all manner of hardships and disappointments. He had focused on building up the body of Christ, especially among the gentiles. He had a clear goal, and he kept the faith.

"I was young and now I am old," says Psalm 37:25. On your own journey, you should set clear goals—and one of those will be saving for retirement. The time will come when your working days are through. You are twenty years old, then thirty, and then, oh my goodness, fifty—and what have you set aside? Nothing? Then you will need to keep working. What once was your dream job may begin to feel like prison. If you start early and set a clear goal of saving for retirement, you can keep out of that prison.

It's not all about money, though. Your path should have a destination. If you are to keep up your pace, you should be striving for something—in fact, a number of things. I believe in concrete planning. It should not be abstract and fuzzy. Here are just a few suggestions of important goals to consider as you build toward something better.

Emergency fund

In every life, some things happen unexpectedly. You should have an emergency fund to handle them. Don't dip into it just because you find a great offer on a new car you desire or you see an advertisement for 30 percent off your dream vacation. Keep the money in your account. Someday you may lose your job, or you or a loved one may face a medical crisis or other sudden need. Your emergency fund will be there to see you through. It will empower you to confidently pursue your other goals—and that sense of security is itself an important goal.

Down payment on a home

Becoming a homeowner is a goal that can provide you and your family with greater stability—but you need to save for it. You will need a substantial down payment, in most cases, and you will also have a variety of other expenses associated with the purchase. For first-time home buyers having the funds set aside for the down payment and closing costs is the biggest obstacle that prevents people from owning their own home.

Vacation

The prospect of having some time to unwind can be quite motivating. We all need to relax. It is a great goal to look forward to treating yourself and your family to some lovely retreat. But vacations are not free. You will need to set aside money, and that likely will involve some degree of sacrifice.

College

Many parents feel that it is their responsibility to save for their children's education, although some believe that the kids, if they are so inclined, should find their own means of paying for that major expense. If you want to pay for your children's education, you must start early. It will take time to build that fund. Although there are many sources of financial aid, your income level could make you ineligible for much of it. If you know that will be the case, you need to start setting aside a portion of your own resources.

Wedding

This could be a huge expense, costing many thousands of dollars if you hold to the tradition of paying for the daughter's wedding and treating her like a princess. Or it could be a more modest expense, depending on what you feel is appropriate. But if paying for that big day is in your future and it is important to you, you should be budgeting a reasonable amount and setting that money aside.

Church donations and endowment

Christians who practice their faith will set aside not only their tithes but also money to support a long-range goal. Donations are essential for church operations—and if you save and invest to become a mighty person of wealth, you could leave an endowment that will serve the Lord's

> purposes for many years to come. Your endowment, for example, could pay for regular counseling and speaking presentations at your church on financial topics. Or you could designate it to support a church leader, perhaps a part-time minister, whose focus would be on developing the finances of the congregation and the church. Your endowment could support a church ministry that you feel called to help develop.

Once you have set your goals, find pictures to help you visualize them. If you are saving for a cruise, get a picture of a cruise ship. If you are saving for a house, find a picture of a lovely home. If your goal is peace of mind, find a picture of something that represents that to you. Having a constant reminder of why you are sacrificing will keep you in focus.

In Hebrews 11:1, we read: "Now faith is the substance of things hoped for, the evidence of things not seen." You are exercising faith that the Lord will provide the ways and means for you to reach your goals. When you look at those pictures, you can say, "The Lord is able, the Lord will provide." So keep the faith, finish the course, and endure to the end.

Visualizing your goals will keep you on track when things become difficult and you are struggling to find your way. It is natural to feel those moments of uncertainty and frustration. Jesus himself, free of sin, struggled at Gethsemane to do what he was sent to do. Don't be distracted from your course. When you find yourself wondering whether you are getting anywhere, look at those pictures. Keep your focus.

If you need an even stronger reminder of why you are sacrificing, take it a step further: Instead of just looking at a picture of your dream home, go to an open house and imagine yourself living in such a setting. If your goal is to marry, go to a wedding parlor and look at the dresses and tuxedos. Or watch a video about that vacation destination for which you are saving, or give yourself some time to sit in a park without a care in the world, just knowing you are on your way to financial security—even if you do not feel that way today.

To become a mighty person of wealth takes time, but do not let that discourage you. With consistency and patience, you will succeed. You may feel that you are moving slowly toward your goal, but that is more than a lot of people accomplish. Small steps are better than no steps.

THE BOTTOM LINE

You can save and invest for multiple goals that are important to you. Success comes from focusing on those goals every day and working toward them diligently, refusing to be discouraged.

CHAPTER 10

RETIREMENT PLANNING

The sluggard will not plow by reason of the cold; therefore shall he beg in harvest, and have nothing.

—Proverbs 20:4

About 75 percent of people age fifty and older are unprepared financially for retirement, according to a 2014 study by AARP.[2] That's a lot of people who are not ready for their golden years. They are heading into a period of life when they finally have the time to do anything—but they won't have the money to do it.

Retirees have told me that their biggest regret was that they did not save for these years—or that they had not saved enough. If you get to age sixty without savings or pension, what retirement options will you have? If you are counting on Social Security, understand that the rules could change. What if Congress raises the retirement age? What if you cannot keep working for health reasons?

2 Alicia Williams and Jonathan Jackson, "2014 Retirement Confidence Survey: A Secondary Analysis of the Findings from Respondents Age 50+," AARP, accessed May 19, 2017, http://www.aarp.org/research/topics/economics/info-2015/retirement-confidence-secondary-analysis.html.

If your vision is a vibrant retirement, living on your own terms, you need to plan now to make that happen. The farmer prepares the soil for the seed, plants it, and cultivates the crop. He does his part, prays about the weather, and leaves the rest to God. Retirement planning is like that. You must do your part and be ready for any weather or, like the proverbial sluggard who would not plow, you will have nothing come harvest time.

Some people live as if they will be young forever. You won't. Yes, it can be hard to think about what will be happening in thirty or forty years, but older people know how quickly the decades can and do pass by. As they near retirement, many have failed to prepare, and it is too late to make up for that lost time. Some knew better, but they found excuses and did nothing. Most of those who failed to prepare for retirement, however, never were taught that the sooner you start saving, even if just a little, the better off you will be.

The Lord wants us to live abundantly—and he wants us to learn and practice the way of life that will lead to that abundance. Are you leading your household on the path of wealth and prosperity? If you are to demonstrate prudent finances to those around you, you need to know where and how to begin. You must understand the fundamentals of a strong, secure retirement. In this chapter, we will examine those building blocks.

SOCIAL SECURITY

"Will Social Security be there for me when I retire?" It's a common question. Many of the millennial generation do not believe they will get that benefit, and yet many of them are doing nothing to prepare for their retirement years.

You should start working with what you know today, and that is your current estimated benefit. Check your statement. The Social Security Administration has cut back on those annual mailings, but you can easily get yours online at https://www.ssa.gov/. It will show your earnings history and give an estimate of the benefit you can expect. The older you are, the more accurate that estimated statement will be.

A recent AARP study found that, on average, about a quarter of the population age sixty-five and older depended on Social Security for 90 percent of their family retirement income.[3] How much will you be depending on that benefit, and how much of it do you expect will be there for you when you retire? If you are counting on Social Security for a significant portion of your retirement income, you should be prepared for the prospect that the government could change the program—and not for the good. So much of that answer does depend on your age group and what other savings plans you are working with to prepare for retirement. That is why it is so critical to have a comprehensive retirement developed for you.

A common and highly complex question about when to begin collecting your benefits—whether at the full retirement age of sixty-six or as early as age sixty-two or as late as age seventy. The younger you are when you claim your benefit, the less you will receive, permanently. If you start your benefit at sixty-two, you face a penalty; how much of a penalty you will face will be based on the year you were born. There were a number of changes to Social Security benefits throughout the life of the program.

---

3 "People Aged 65 and Older Who Rely on Social Security for 90% of Family Income (in 2013) and Average Monthly Benefit (December, 2014) by State," Public Policy Institute, November 12, 2015, http://www.aarp.org/ppi/info-2015/people-aged-65-and-older-who-rely-on-social-security-for-90-percent-of-family-income-and-average-monthly-benefit-by-state.html.

Your full retirement age depends on the year you were born. Currently it is sixty-six for those born from 1943 through 1954. It is sixty-seven for those born 1960 or later. For those born between those years, full retirement age rises by two months every year. For example, if you were born in 1955, your full retirement age is sixty-six years and two months; if you were born in 1959, it is sixty-six years and ten months. The government has changed the full retirement age in the past, and it could do so again.

The following chart illustrates the monthly benefits at ages sixty-two, sixty-four, sixty-seven, and seventy. As you can see from the example, a person who would receive $1,000 per month at their full retirement age would receive substantially less if he or she decided to receive their benefits early. Those who can delay receiving their benefits can get a lot more. These figures will differ slightly for those whose full retirement age is earlier. You should check with the SSA to check for what specifically applies to you.

AGE 62 (EARLY BENEFIT)	AGE 64 (STILL EARLY BENEFIT)	AGE 67 (FULL RETIREMENT AGE)	AGE 70 (DELAY RETIREMENT AGE)
$700 per month	$800 per month	$1,000 per month	$1,300 per month

PENSION

Whether you will have a pension as a building block for retirement is highly questionable, but I include it here because it is still an important element for some. Although many current retirees still collect that lifelong stream of monthly income from their former employer, very few companies today offer this benefit. Those that do may require that you work there for a period of time, perhaps a decade or even thirty years, before you are eligible to receive your pension at the age determined by the plan. I am talking about original employer-based pensions where the employer is responsible for everything in the plan and you just receive a monthly check when you retire. The main individuals who receive this traditional benefit primarily work for the government on a federal, state, city, or local level.

If you participate in a 401(k) plan with your employer, understand that it is not a pension. In a pension, investments are the responsibility of the employer. In a 401(k), the employee chooses the investments from a menu of offerings. Since the 1980s, many companies have dropped their pension plans and replaced them with 401(k) plans—and that represents a major shift in the focus of retirement planning. It has become the responsibility of the individual, not the employer, to invest wisely for retirement.

If you do have a pension, the size of your benefit will depend on how long you were employed, how much you earned, and how long you participated in the pension plan. It is not unusual that people forget about a pension they could claim from a job they left years earlier. They moved on, but the pension account was still active. It's worth the time to track it down. For one client, it took six months of letters and phone calls, but we were able to locate her pension and get the benefit in place.

RETIREMENT ACCOUNTS

They are called retirement accounts because you are expected to wait until that time of life before withdrawing the money. If you take it out too early, the IRS will penalize you.

There are a variety of such plans, but let's start with a closer look at the 401(k) that many employers offer. As an employee, you put money into the account to grow for use when you are older. Some companies will match what you put in. For example, you contribute 6 percent of your salary, and the company adds 3 percent. That means a $600 contribution brings you $300 in free money. That's a 50 percent return on your investment right at the start. It is a great benefit, but many people let that free money go. They fail to put in enough money to get the full match. How many of you are letting free money slip away?

Nonprofit companies call these plans 403(b)s, but they operate much the same. For government workers, they are called 457 plans. The rules are slightly different, but the concept is the same. Your biggest asset is time. Through the years, your investments in these plans should overcome the ups and downs of the market.

Now let's look at how a traditional 401(k)-type plan operates, as compared to the Roth 401(k) option that some employers offer. In a traditional plan, you can deduct from your income the amount that you contribute. That produces an immediate savings because it lowers your taxable income each year. However, when you withdraw your money from the account during retirement, you must pay income tax then on the amount of the withdrawal, which will include what you contributed and what your investments earned.

The Roth differs in that you do not get that immediate tax savings. You pay all your income tax upfront before contributing to the account. However, you are never taxed on that money again or on the amount that it grows. In retirement, you withdraw it free of taxes.

In other words, the traditional plan is "tax me later but not now," and the Roth plan is "tax me now but not later." Which is best? It depends on your financial situation. Let's look at an example of how the two compare.

TRADITIONAL ("TAX ME LATER BUT NOT NOW.")	ROTH ("TAX ME NOW BUT NOT LATER.")
$35,000 your gross income –$5,000 your 401(k) contribution $30,000 remaining after contribution	$35,000 your gross income –$5,000 your Roth contribution $30,000 remaining after contribution
$30,000 your taxable income –$6,000 immediate tax due at 20% rate $24,000 what's left for you ($30,000–$6,000)	$35,000 your taxable income –$7,000 immediate tax due at 20% rate $23,000 what's left for you ($30,000–$7,000)

It would appear from that chart that the traditional plan is the way to go, hands down. However, thirty years later the Roth makes a stunning comeback. You now can withdraw your contributions and your earnings free of taxes—and as you can see in the next chart, that makes a huge difference in your wealth.

TRADITIONAL	ROTH
$30,000 amount of withdrawal –$6,000 tax due at 20% rate $24,000 amount remaining	$30,000 amount of withdrawal 0 no taxes due $30,000 amount remaining

There is much to consider before choosing between a traditional plan or a Roth—or perhaps investing in both. Will you be better off saving on taxes up front, so that you might have more to invest through the years, or saving on taxes way down the road? Do you need that upfront tax savings to meet your daily expenses? Or do you want the peace of mind of knowing that you will have retirement income that is tax-free? Which will better enhance your lifestyle?

Your financial advisor can help you with those considerations and calculations so that you can make the decision that is best for you and your family. Just know that, either way, you are on a path of saving and investing, and that is what will make all the difference.

If you are self-employed, you have options as well. You can set up a retirement account for yourself; you can do a Solo 401(k), or you can set up a SEP account or a Keogh account for your business. There are many online sources where you can learn the details of how these plans work and the rules you must comply with. Do your homework and speak with a professional if you are interested in one of these retirement plans. In this "gig economy" age, it will be extremely important to utilize one of these retirement accounts.

An individual retirement account (IRA) is another way to save for retirement if you or your spouse have earned income from a job. You can put your money into an IRA and get your tax deduction as late as the final day of the tax season, which usually is April 15. Your tax professional can tell you how much you can contribute to an IRA and to the other retirement plan options. The IRA offers the same choices as a 401(k): you can open a traditional plan for the upfront tax savings or a Roth for the tax-free withdrawals.

YOUR TAXABLE INVESTMENT ACCOUNT

Another building block for retirement is the money that you invest in your own portfolio outside of those retirement plans that we just examined. You might think of this as "money I can touch," because your preretirement access is not restricted. You will want to do more with your money than just keep it in a bank savings account—otherwise, you might as well stuff it in your mattress because it will not be earning enough to keep up with inflation. You need to get your money working for you.

That means opening a taxable investment account. You will pay taxes on your gains, so if you get a hot tip and buy a stock at $19 a share and sell it at $100, you will be responsible for $81 in capital gains taxes—either at the short-term rate if you have held the stock for under a year or the long-term rate if you have held it for more than a year. You should aim for long-term capital gains, which allow you to keep more of your money.

INVESTMENT REAL ESTATE

Property can be a great investment, although being a landlord can bring you headaches and sleepless nights. You have probably seen television shows about flipping houses for profit—for example, buying a house for $100,000, doing $25,000 worth of work, and then selling it for $175,000, making a $50,000 profit. People do make money that way, but it's not for everyone. For most, real estate investing means the tried, true, and boring approach. You buy a piece of property, rent it out for twenty or thirty years while it produces a stream of income for you each month, and then sell it at a profit.

PUTTING IT ALL TOGETHER

As you look at all those building blocks, you will need to figure out whether they are sufficient to construct your retirement. How sturdy are those blocks? And are they all there? As we have seen, the pension block may be missing entirely, and Social Security benefits could change, particularly for younger people. You have to prepare and prepare now.

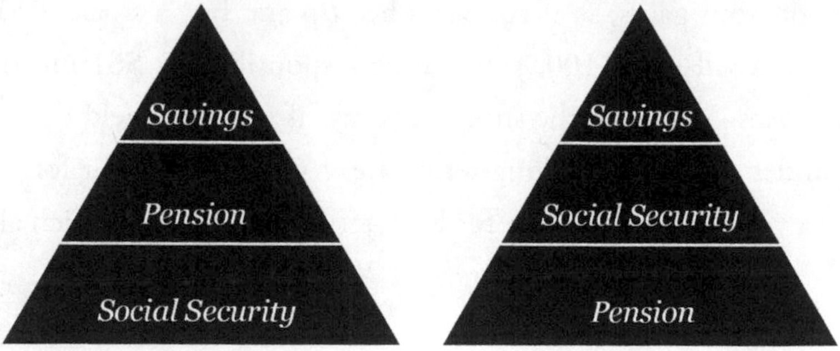

Don't let your golden years turn into tinfoil. It's time to wake up to the important task of planning for retirement. Young people should take action without delay, while they have time—and while the power of that time is on their side. But even if you are starting late, at least you are starting. Don't become one of those who live in fear during their retirement years. It is time to put your hands to the plow and take charge of your life and your finances.

THE BOTTOM LINE

God wants us to live abundantly, but he expects us to keep our hands to the plow, picking up and using the tools that he provides. Long before you retire, you need to design an income plan from various sources that will see you and your family through. It's never too late to take charge of your finances.

CHAPTER 11

KEY INVESTMENT CONCEPTS

Wisdom is the principal thing; therefore get wisdom: and with all thy getting get understanding.

—Proverbs 4:7

"What's the worst that can happen?" people often ask when deciding whether to take a chance on something. That is the essence of risk management. Many aspects of our lives involve some form of risk. Things happen that an individual, or a business, cannot control. A new technology hits the market, for example, and makes a product or service obsolete. A loved one slips in the bathtub and is seriously injured. A crash on the highway claims a life. You are at risk even when you cross the street while following all the rules.

Though you cannot control all that happens, you certainly can take precautions, and you can plan for the possibility that the worst will happen. That way you will have the resources to deal with it, come what may. Risks are part of life. You must manage them, but you cannot stay in bed all day for fear that something bad might happen to you. Because things can happen to you there too.

Risk management is a key concept in successful investment. In your financial decisions, you need to understand risk and how to minimize it. Every investment, even a US Treasury bond, has an element of risk. The question to ask yourself is how much risk you can accept.

As with other risks, you cannot live in fear over everything that could possibly happen. You must use facts and logic to make your best decisions and to manage your investment risk, but even when you follow all the rules, things can go wrong—just as they can when you cross the street. That does not mean you must not invest, any more than it means you must never cross the street. Investing is truly a choice—and how you deal with the inherent risks is also your choice.

Just remember that millions of people have successfully invested for their future and are now enjoying the fruits of their long-term strategy. Most went through bad patches in the market—and you will too—but they stuck it out. They held on. Despite its ups and downs, the market rises over time.

Yes, you can get killed crossing the street. Thousands of people also die in car crashes each year. But even knowing all that, you will probably still want to take walks and still want to drive. When you choose to drive instead of walk, you are exchanging one set of risks for another. That's how it is with investing. You are choosing one set of risk factors over another—and your choice will differ from what others do. You must understand your own rationale for your decisions.

INVESTING TO OVERCOME INFLATION

To demonstrate the function of risk in your investment choices, think about the rising cost of a movie ticket. Not all that long ago, a movie ticket in New York City was $10. Today it's about $20, and it may well double to $40 in thirty years due to inflation. The increase in the cost of goods and services, which over the past century has averaged about 3 percent a year, is the normal result of economic growth and expansion. In 1970, for example, gasoline averaged thirty-six cents a gallon, a loaf of bread cost a quarter, and the average price of a new home was $23,450. Though it is normal, inflation must not be ignored. You need to save and invest so that you not only keep up with inflation but outpace it so it does not eat away at your standard of living.

How, then, can you invest $20 today so that it has the best chance of becoming the $40 that you will need for a movie in thirty years?

Let's look at the hypothetical results of three investment approaches: (a) the "mattress" strategy, (b) the US Treasuries strategy, and (c) the stock strategy. As you can see in the chart, your $20 investment will yield different results:

AMOUNT INVESTED	INVESTMENT STRATEGY	RESULT
$20	The mattress	$20
$20	US Treasuries	$30
$20	Stocks	$40

In the mattress strategy (a), you stuff your $20 in the mattress. The benefit: In three decades, you will still have your $20, although not a penny more. The risk: You can't go to the movies. The solution: You need to find an additional $20 somewhere.

In the US Treasuries strategy (b), you buy a long-term bond. The benefit: You feel virtually certain that the government will pay you the $10 in interest as promised and then return your $20. The risk: You will only have $30, still not enough to see a movie. The solution: You need to find an additional $10 somewhere.

In the stocks strategy (c), you invest your $20 in the market. The benefit: Ideally, it will grow to the $40 that you need. The risk: It might not, and you could even lose money. The solution: You can follow a diversified and balanced investment strategy with a broad stock index fund. You are not trying to beat the market—just trying to keep up.

With each of those strategies, you have some sort of risk. You need to decide which you will accept. Stuffing your mattress gives you no growth. Bonds might not give you enough growth to meet your needs. With stocks, you must endure the ups and downs of the market—but at least you do have the potential to meet and or even exceed your financial goals.

INVESTING VS. SAVING

Saving and investing are different disciplines with different purposes, and what primarily differentiates them is that investing involves more risk. Saving is simply putting money aside for later use. For example, if you need it for an emergency or whatever purpose, you can walk into the bank and withdraw the money that you have saved. If you have $5,000.01 in the bank (the .01 is the interest you received on your money), it will be waiting there for you whenever you want to withdraw it. You need not worry that you will only have $4,500, as might be the case if you invested your money in the stock market.

When should you save rather than invest? Generally, you should save if you will need the money within five years. For example, if you have $30,000 and know that you will need it for a down payment on a house in five years, you generally should put that money in savings rather than investments. If you invest it, you could lose some of it. You should not take that risk with money that you know you will need relatively soon.

In other words, the difference between saving and investing is that, when you invest, you are accepting a degree of risk so that you have the potential to make more money. Let's say you won't need that $30,000 for a down payment until ten years from now. You might see it fall to $10,000—and then so much for your down payment. Or you might invest $15,000 and see it double to what you need over the next ten years with a prudent investment strategy.

INTEREST AND COMPOUNDING

Interest is basically what you are compensated for lending your money. When you lend money to a person or an entity, you are saying that you believe in them. You have faith that they will return your hard-earned money to you as promised.

When you reinvest that interest, it compounds. As your account grows, you are putting to work not only your principal but also the amount that it has earned. Over time, compounding can dramatically increase your wealth, so the sooner you start, the better. How often the money is compounded also makes a big difference. Let's say one company will pay you 10 percent once per year, and another will pay you 2.5 percent every three months. At the end of the first year, your earnings would look like this:

$100 + 10% = $110
$100 + 2.5% = $102.50 + 2.5% = $105.06 + 2.5% = $107.69 + 2.5% = $110.38

As you can see, when interest compounds quarterly, your money grows faster. Over time, that becomes a big difference. Here's how $20,000 compounded annually for thirty years compares to the same amount compounded quarterly for thirty years:

$20,000 × 10% compounded yearly for 30 years = $348,988.05

$20,000 × 10% compounded quarterly for 30 years = $387,163.00

That's nearly $40,000 produced simply by the quarterly compounding. I'm sure you could think of some uses for that money. That is why it is so important to start investing as soon as possible. When you combine time with compounding, you have a powerhouse investment strategy.

MARKET CYCLES

What goes up must come down—a truth in many things, including investing. In the recent housing crisis, many homeowners saw that truth play out in a drastic way. But economic cycles such as that are natural. In the housing market, there are times when there are more buyers and times when there are more sellers. There are times of loss and times of opportunity.

I think of Harlem in New York City, which was so depressed for decades that you could buy interesting properties for as little as $50,000. Today, properties are selling there easily for $1 million and more. As people flock to a hot market, it gets hotter—and vice versa. Whether you are in a good situation or a bad one will depend on whether you are a buyer or a seller and whether the market is at its peak or at its bottom.

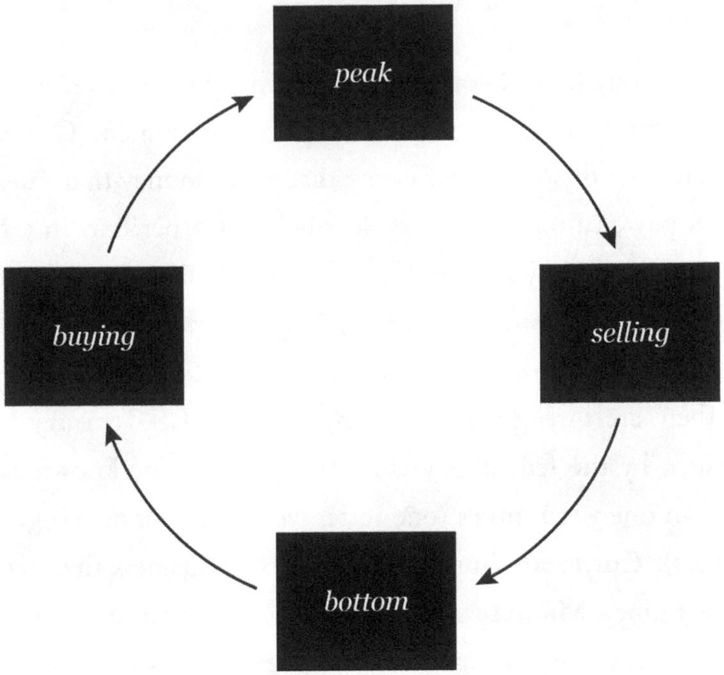

There are also cycles in the stock market, in individual stocks, in real estate and business, and in trends of many kinds. If you are an investor, so much depends on where you are when you start to buy. If you buy at the peak, you soon will have to endure the selling as the market begins to cycle down and you become increasingly depressed about the losses. If you buy at the bottom, you are coming in at bargain prices and getting great value for your money. As more buyers join you, prices rise with the demand. Many investors, though, get the timing wrong. They buy high during the excitement and sell low when they are feeling depressed about their investment decisions. Letting emotions dictate their buying and selling is what leads many investors astray.

BONDS

When you buy bonds, you are lending money to whoever issues the bonds. It might be the federal, state, or local government. Or it might be a company or some other entity that raises money that way. Let's say you pay $1,000 for a thirty-year bond at 5 percent. In essence, the issuer is telling you this: *If you lend me $1,000 for thirty years, I will give you 5 percent, or $50, every year for three decades, and at the end of the thirtieth year I will give you your $1,000 back.*

There are three principal types of bonds. **US Treasury bonds** are issued by the federal government. Treasuries are known as bills (less than one year), notes (one to ten years), or bonds (longer than ten years). **Corporate bonds** are issued by a business that needs to borrow money. **Municipal bonds** are issued by a government entity. Generally, you are not taxed on what they earn for you; if they are "triple tax-free," neither the federal, state, or local government will tax you.

DIVERSIFICATION

Diversification is a way to manage the risk of investing in stocks and bonds. To borrow an old saying, it means that all your eggs are not in one basket. By diversifying, you strive to maintain balance in your investments. Ideally, when your portfolio is diversified, one stock will be rising while another is struggling, keeping you in balance through the cycles. Or perhaps if your stocks in general are down, then your bonds might be doing well.

Knowing that you have that balance can give you the peace of mind to sleep well at night even in a tough market. Let's look at some of the ways that diversification can be accomplished.

MUTUAL AND INDEX FUNDS

Mutual funds will allow you to instantly diversify without a lot of cash. They provide "professional" management of your stocks. Fund managers have the time and resources to evaluate individual stocks and industries more than the average person, with the goal of producing a return that is better than that of the overall market. That is hard to do—in fact, most mutual funds do not reach that goal.

When you buy a mutual fund, you become the part owner of a basket of stocks that can help to balance your investments. For that service, you pay a management fee to the mutual fund company. In recent years there have been more than nine thousand funds to choose from. In most 401(k)-type plans, mutual funds are the only way you can invest your money in the market.

You can choose from a variety of funds. There are funds that focus on energy stocks, bonds, the health care sector, and foreign stock market, to name a few.

An index fund is a type of mutual fund that tries to match the performance of market indices.

Index funds do not try to do better than the overall stock market. Instead, they take the approach of "if you can't beat them, join them." If the overall market is up 9 percent, the goal of an index fund is to be as close to that 9 percent as possible. If it charges a 1 percent management fee, the mutual fund therefore will have to earn 10 percent just to be equal to the overall market.

The advantage that index funds have over other mutual funds is their low management fees. Because it is managed by a computer and the primary goal is to be equal to the market, the fund can charge very low fees—for example, 0.2 percent, or two cents on $100. Just like mutual funds, you can choose different types—banking, telecommunications, and industrial index funds, for example.

DIVIDENDS

A dividend is a stream of money that some companies will pay you when you own their stock. As a stockholder, or shareholder, you essentially are a part owner of the company, and so you are sharing in its fortunes. Many investors, as well as mutual funds, focus only on dividend-paying companies.

If you are a first-time investor, you may find dividend-paying stocks particularly attractive because you know that your money is always working for you. If the stock market falls and you get your dividend, all of a sudden your money can buy more shares. You're sad that the stock has dropped, of course, but you're happy that you have more shares. If the stock rises, you're happy about that even though you get fewer shares for your money. You are always in a win-win situation, and you always see some sort of growth in your account. That's important for first-time investors who are still not quite sure about the market and how it works.

CERTIFICATES OF DEPOSIT (CDs)

A CD is best thought of as a supercharged savings account with money you do not expect to need while it is locked up. Historically, CDs have never produced a return that quite kept up with the inflation rate, so they alone will not provide sufficient growth for your investment portfolio. Why have them at all, then? Because CDs are designed for another purpose, and they may fit your needs perfectly.

Let's say you plan to buy a car but definitely not for two years. You can buy a CD with a two-year term and earn more interest than you would get from letting your money sit in a bank savings account, without running a risk of losing any of it. Likewise, if you know you will need a down payment for a house in five years, you can buy a CD with a five-year term. In both cases, a CD would serve your short-term purpose. Even though it would be no match for inflation over the long term, at least you would not be stuffing your money in a mattress earning nothing.

In the recent low interest rate environment, the interest on your money has been relatively minimal, but CDs have still paid more than a regular savings account. You can open a CD for as little as three months or as long as ten years. If you want your money before the term is up, however, and cancel your contract, you will forfeit the promised earnings.

DOLLAR COST AVERAGING

For investors, dollar cost averaging is the great equalizer. If you are regularly investing a set sum of money over time, such as with 401(k) contributions, and continue to do so whether the market is up or down, you can benefit greatly from this concept. Let's say you have $400 to invest in a company that you believe will do well. You decide to invest $100 every month for four months. Here is an example of the results of such dollar cost averaging, compared with investing the $400 as a lump sum.

DCA	LUMP SUM
$100 @ $30 per share = 3.33 shares	$400 @ $30 per share = 13.33
$100 @ $19 per share = 5.26 shares	
$100 @ $26 per share = 3.84 shares	
$100 @ $23 per share = 4.34 shares	
Avg. $24.50 per share; Total shares = 16.77	Avg. $30 per share; Total shares = 13.33
16.77 × $60 = $1,006	13.33 × $60 = $800

As you can see, investing through dollar cost averaging gives you better results in this example. You end up with more shares at a lower average price. If you had invested the $400 as a lump sum when the price was $30, you might have been tempted to sell at a loss when the price dropped to $19. Instead, you kept up your regular monthly purchases, and instead of selling low, you bought low. And in the end, with a sale price of $60, you didn't miss out on those lower bargain prices. You ended up $200 ahead.

No strategy works all the time. Dollar cost averaging is not the best approach in a rising market. It is at its best when you keep buying even when prices fall, obtaining more shares as in the example. In a rising market, lump sum investment makes more sense because you are locking in your money at a lower price point. But over the long term, as the market cycles up and down through the years, dollar cost averaging can be highly advantageous.

DO NOT BE DISCOURAGED

Along your new path, as you use these concepts and principles toward the goal of financial empowerment, you will run into the disillusioned and the defeated. Because misery loves company, some will try to discourage you. "Investing is a sucker's game," they will say. "It's geared for the rich, and it's just too risky." Don't let them pull you down into the darkness with those lies.

When a good farmer experiences a year of drought, he does not tell all the other farmers to just give up. Experienced farmers understand that some years bring a poor harvest, and they learn better ways to overcome and manage. Farmers encourage, support, and share information with one another, especially with the young farmers.

They do not forsake the land, just as experienced investors do not forsake the market.

Most of the media attention on stocks comes during two vulnerable points in the market cycle—at its peak, when everyone is excited and new investors are pouring in, and when it's close to the bottom of the sell-off and you hear the horror stories of money lost while "investing." Many people get their introduction to the market when they are lured in when the market is at or just past the peak in the cycle. Then they watch with dismay as the market drifts to the bottom, when they become so discouraged that they bail out. They buy high, sell low, and lose out. They give up just when they should be bargain hunting.

Many of the market naysayers have had that sort of bad experience. They are the ones who would discourage you on your quest to become a mighty person of wealth. They can make you feel as if you should just spend your money and deal with the fallout later. Ask them what they do with their own money, if they do not invest it in the market. Money, like water, will flow somewhere. Are they into real estate? That can be a sound strategy. Treasury bonds? Certificates of deposit? Even if they just put it in the bank for a tiny bit of interest because they are not sure what to do, that would be a start. But if they are doing none of that, you have to wonder whether they are just looking for an excuse to go back to their spendthrift ways.

If you have come to believe that investing is like gambling or that it only benefits the wealthy, ask yourself, how did you form those impressions? Did family members talk negatively about the market? Did a friend tell you bitterly how he or she was swindled? Give it some thought. Learning to invest wisely is part of digging your strong foundation. You can fight off those negative feelings with the facts. You can put down some of that baggage and travel more lightly.

It takes time to get it right. When you first came to know Christ, were you a mature Christian on day one? New believers seldom act from the start as if they have walked with the Lord for decades. They will face many trials and much testing of their spiritual strength, and they need encouragement rather than criticism. As you grow in your financial strength, you will not be perfect. This, too, is a lifelong journey, and you will have lessons to learn and obstacles to overcome.

King David had failures along this path, but "he died in a good old age, full of days, riches, and honor." As a Christian, you will gain wealth through honest and fair investments and other financial dealings. If you operate a business, you can do quite well by providing excellent service and goods at a fair price to your customers. As you glorify the Lord, and as you do your part, you will be on your way to abundant living.

THE BOTTOM LINE

To get ahead financially, you should do more than save. You need to put those dollars to work for you by investing them for a return that will keep ahead of inflation.

CHAPTER 12

RENTING VS. BUYING

Through wisdom a house is built, and by understanding it is established; by knowledge the rooms are filled with all precious and pleasant riches.

—Proverbs 24:3–4

Some people preach that everyone should own a home. That is a sweeping generalization, and it is just not true. Not everyone has the temperament for homeownership. Nor is it true that it makes more sense to rent than to own. Here's the truth—it all depends. Many factors will determine whether buying a home is right for you.

I do strongly believe in homeownership and its benefits, but I recognize that it is not always in the best interest of the individual or the family. You will need to come to this decision for yourself, so let's look at some considerations.

Your first question should be why do you want to take this step. What does homeownership mean to you? Perhaps you see it as a symbol of status, of freedom, or of financial opportunity. Maybe you need room for a growing family, and paying rent feels as if you are throwing money away. Whatever your reasons, take time to identify why homeownership is important to you. You need to fully understand its advantages and disadvantages to determine whether it is an experience that will fulfill your expectations.

ADVANTAGES OF OWNING A HOME

A big advantage of homeownership is the ability of real estate to gain value over the years. Think of it, though, as a long-term investment, not as some kind of get-rich-quick scheme.

I bought a co-op in 1989 at a peak in the real estate market. In 1990, the market crashed—I paid $50,000 for the property, and it was then appraised at $20,000. Nonetheless, I kept faithfully paying my mortgage. Twelve years later, my property was worth $100,000. It took time, but the value eventually doubled.

I bought that property before the home-as-an-investment craze that changed how people thought about homeownership. Today, many people would feel pressured to get rid of such a property when it has lost so much value, figuring that the "investment" just hasn't worked out. If that's how you think of your home—that it is just an investment in the strictest sense of the word—then when your investment falls 60 percent you should probably sell.

Many people have bought a home with an unreasonable expectation that they can pay, say, $300,000 now and their investment will grow to $500,000 in two years. They are not thinking of owning a home in the traditional sense of a good place to live for many years while it steadily gains value as they pay off the mortgage. They are just focusing on the investment angle.

Different factors drive every housing market. Here in New York City, the dynamic housing economy is far different than in many areas of the country. If you are considering homeownership, you should learn about the market in the area you would be buying into. What makes it different from other areas? Do some research. You can learn a great deal online or at seminars sponsored by your local bank.

Another advantage of homeownership is the sense of security you get from knowing that, so long as you do your part financially, you and your family will have a roof over your heads. You can know that your monthly housing expense will be relatively stable—that is, if you have a fixed-rate mortgage, which is generally in your best interest. A big variable might be the real estate taxes, which at times could rise dramatically, but generally you can know that the basic expense will be steady. You will not have a landlord deciding to boost the rent higher year after year or a sudden jump in rent when a dramatic shift in the neighborhood enables the landlord to charge more.

Meanwhile, you will be building equity. In other words, the home will be worth increasingly more than the remaining mortgage. For example, if your home is now worth $300,000 and you have a remaining mortgage of only $150,000, you would have $150,000 in equity if you were to sell. If you keep your home until you have made all the mortgage payments, you will have 100 percent equity in it. All that added value is yours. It's old-fashioned homeownership savings.

You can tap into that equity without selling your house, if you wish. You can borrow against the equity or refinance your property to pull some of it out in cash. Be careful if you refinance, however, and be clear about what you are doing. Let's say your home is worth $350,000 and you have a mortgage remaining of $150,000. By refinancing, you could pull out a percentage of your equity, perhaps as much as $165,000. What you are doing is starting over with another thirty-year mortgage—and now you will owe $315,000 (which is the amount you still owed, plus the amount you pulled out in cash). Is that really what you want to do? Instead, you could ask the bank for a loan—say, $50,000 over ten years—based on the extra value of your property. Remember, this is how a number of people lost their home during the recent housing bubble.

There are good and legitimate reasons to refinance. You can get a lower interest rate, and that can be a worthy goal if you plan to stay in the house long enough to justify the refinancing fees and expenses. Perhaps you plan to use the money for improvements that will significantly enhance the value of your home. My caution, once again, is this: you should not be using your house as some kind of ATM that dispenses magical money. Those are real dollars, and you must handle that added debt wisely.

Homeownership also comes with potential tax benefits. When you itemize and file the long form, you can deduct your mortgage interest and your property taxes on your return. Those deductions can have a powerful effect on your family budget. Those tax breaks mean that the government is subsidizing homeownership to encourage people to become homeowners. I have shown people, after working out the tax savings, that for the rent they are paying, or a little bit more, they can own their own home.

When you own your home, you attain an added level of security if you go through some rough times, such as losing your job. In New York City, for example, a lot of people who rent feel a sense of insecurity: What would they do, for example, if the landlord were to sell the property and kick them out? As a homeowner, you have more control. Although you are still obligated to pay the mortgage, of course, it is unlikely that you would be quickly and summarily booted from your residence if you miss a payment or two. That's a serious situation, but at least you would have a greater level of stability and more time to reorganize your finances.

Homeownership can provide that solid sense of stability and reliability to you and your family. Your home and its value can become part of your legacy that you leave to your children and grandchildren. Owning your home can be rewarding psychologically as well as financially. Your home is your castle. You could paint your living room hot pink if you wanted, without worrying that your landlord would keep your security deposit. You can poke all the holes you want in the walls to hang whatever you wish. You gain a greater sense of privacy, and you have the freedom and pride of ownership. Only you can say how important those factors are to you.

DISADVANTAGES OF HOMEOWNERSHIP

When buying a house, you may have difficulty coming up with a down payment and closing costs, which is the expense of borrowing the money. The lender also will want you to establish that you have sufficient money to make your payments even if you experience an emergency of some sort.

Homeownership should be fulfilling. It should make you happy, not stressed—some who have taken that step find that they have overstretched themselves. They can come to feel as if all their work and efforts are on behalf of the house. You need to assess all the costs of owning a house and see where they will fit on your family budget. If you cannot find room for everything that matters, you are not ready. Renting could be your best option.

One of the costs of owning a house is maintenance and repairs. Some things need to be done regularly—mowing, gutter cleaning, hedge trimming, snowplowing, painting, etc.—and things will inevitably break down: "What? My water heater must be replaced?" You have to anticipate problems like that now and then, and some repairs are expensive. You need to be ready. You might have the skills to do some of the repairs and maintenance yourself, and you might even like to come home from a hard day's work for the joy of doing more work. But whether you do the work yourself or hire someone, you still need to get that expense into your budget.

When you own a home, you are locking yourself into a long-term obligation. If your life plans change and you need to sell, it can take a long time—in fact, some buyers will offer you less if they know you're in a hurry to sell. It's the same if you discover that you simply do not like the neighborhood, so you should find out all you can about it beforehand. You should think of a home purchase as a commitment to live in an area for quite some time.

And when it does come time to sell your home, you have no guarantee that you will make a profit. Most homes in most markets have increased in value over time, but you can find many examples of markets around the country where the economic conditions have sent values plunging. Many people in the recent housing crisis found that their home was worth far less than they paid for it, and yet they were still obligated to the mortgage. That should not sour you on the prospect of owning a home, however, particularly if you are in it for the long haul and think through every angle before your purchase.

DISADVANTAGES OF RENTING

One of the big disadvantages of renting your home is that you are building no equity. In effect, you are paying the mortgage for the landlord, but the landlord keeps all the gain in the home's value. Renting can be cheaper than a home mortgage and the associated costs but not necessarily. A lot depends on what you are renting and where. Try to rent a true three-bedroom apartment in New York City, and you will see what I mean.

You are also at risk of those annual rent increases. Those can be especially tough if you are in an area that is becoming gentrified. Gentrification is the cost of living in a neighborhood rising dramatically because it has become increasingly attractive to people who are willing and able to pay a lot more to live there. If you are paying $1,000 a month and your neighborhood is gentrifying, your landlord may soon want $2,000 a month. In any rental situation, though, over time your monthly payments are likely to rise. You will not have the price stability that you generally would get with homeownership.

Renters do not get the savings opportunity that a homebuyer gets. One young man told me that he was renting for $1,200 and did not see the point of buying a home and paying $2,200. I pointed out that homeownership amounts to built-in savings, and otherwise he should be setting aside $1,000 per month in savings and $700 more for retirement. "I don't think that's going to be happening," he said. I told him that is why owning a property can be a powerful way to save for the future.

Nor do renters receive any significant advantages when they file their income tax returns, although some states do provide a small renter's credit. They get nothing like the mortgage interest deduction that saves homeowners so much in taxes when they file the long form.

Too many renters do not have the sense of security that homeowners get from knowing that they are in full control of what happens with their property. If you are renting, what do you do if the owner decides to sell the place—and doesn't want any tenants on the premises in the meantime? What do you do if the landlord decides not to renew your contract? Or decides to let a relative live there instead of you? You just got kicked out of your home even though you pay your rent every month. And if you run into financial difficulties, you easily could be evicted, although tenants do have certain protections depending on the state and community.

ADVANTAGES OF RENTING

For many people, renting will continue to be the best option until they are financially positioned for a purchase. A lot of people struggle to come up with the down payment to buy a home, which traditionally is 20 percent of the purchase price but can be as low as 5 percent for conventional mortgages and even less through FHA and other special financing programs. You do not need to come up with that much money to rent, although you generally will need enough for a security deposit and may need to pay both your first and last month's rent in advance.

Your monthly rent often will be less than monthly mortgage payments, although, again, you are not building equity so you should be saving additional money for retirement and other life events. That should be easier for you to do since you won't have the additional overhead expenses of homeownership.

A big advantage to renting is that you do not have the repair and maintenance headaches that a homeowner faces. If the toilet or sink is backed up, you just call the landlord. No heat or hot water? You call the landlord. You wake up on a snowy morning and—ideally—the driveway will be all cleared and salted.

When renting, if you decide that you made a mistake or the neighborhood is no longer to your liking, it is easier to move, although you will need to fulfill your contract obligations. You may be able to work out a payment agreement with your landlord or perhaps find someone to sublet the premises, but expect that you will be responsible for the remaining months of your lease. If you face a life emergency and need to leave the area, at least you will not need to worry about selling your home or finding a tenant so you can afford the mortgage payments. Not everyone is cut out to become a landlord.

YOUR CHOICE NOW

Those are some of the key considerations in deciding whether to rent or buy. As you might imagine, the considerations can get more involved and complex. Some people may want and need a spreadsheet analysis, but remember that you should not think of the purchase of a home as strictly a dollar investment. Be mindful of your motivations for buying or renting. Consider all the pros and cons before deciding what is best for you and your family.

THE BOTTOM LINE

Should you rent or should you buy a home? Each has its advantages and disadvantages—but remember that your choice of a home involves much more than a dollar investment. It's a personal choice that reflects what is important to you.

CHAPTER 13

BUILDING YOUR CAREER

I will instruct thee and teach thee in the way which thou shalt go: I will guide thee with mine eye.

—Psalm 32:8

In our discussions on saving and investment and good financial habits, you may have been thinking that your real issue is that you need more income—and for some people, that is absolutely true. Before reaching that conclusion, I would want to take some time with you to review your earnings and your spending. You can be sure that some people who make less than you still manage to save something.

Let's start with the premise, though, that you are one of those people who does need more income, and until you get it, no amount of budgeting will help your situation. After reading this chapter, you can find a career center in your area sponsored by your state or local government. Local colleges and nonprofits could also offer assistance. First, let's consider some steps that can save you time and get you on your way.

So many things can hinder people from progressing along a career path. A lot depends on your life circumstances, which differ for everyone. I know this: if you have gotten this far in this book, you are motivated to take charge of your finances, and you are willing to put in the time required. That is a big deal. It demonstrates your commitment.

A MATTER OF COMMITMENT

I have met many young people who are single and responsible only for themselves, and their biggest hurdle often is that they do not know what they want to do. They would like to find meaningful employment, but what if it takes twenty years to figure it out? That is not uncommon. I ask them what they are prepared to do now until they figure out what they really want to do.

If that describes you, it is time to commit. You need to apply yourself to a career or job path that will bring in more income now. You should focus your energy and your commitment on learning, and you must not brush things off because you are not interested. Never use that as an excuse for failing to apply yourself. Failure is not an option. You need to start earning a higher salary now, and then later, when you figure out your true calling, you can go down that path.

I recently chatted with a young man in his early twenties who was unsure what he wanted to do for a career. He did know that college wasn't for him at this time, and I agreed. He seemed surprised that I wasn't beating the college drum. I encouraged him to consider a trade. Electricians, for example, earn good money, and they often make extra income on weekends doing jobs for family and friends.

Many people fail when trying to learn a trade, I told him, because they lack two fundamental skills: the ability to show up for work every day and on time, demonstrating that they are reliable; and the ability to come to work prepared to do their best, not drunk, high, or hung over. They make it abundantly clear that they are not interested in what they're doing.

True, he might not be interested in such a trade for the long haul, but it would provide a good income as he searched for his niche. Even if he never found his dream job or vocation, he would still be making excellent money. Learning a trade puts people in a no-lose situation while they work things through. Even as they are trying to figure out their path in life, they still need to commit to something—and the way to commit is to apply yourself to the task at hand, without excuses. I met with that young man a month later, and he had registered with an excellent program to become a car mechanic. Every car owner wants to know a good car mechanic.

What are you willing to do? In talking with many people of a variety of ages through the years, I have found that to be the central question that must be addressed. Only you know whether you are the sort who will do what it takes. If you are not willing to commit to something now, be careful not to waste your time and money developing a career that you will not be committed to learn.

DOING WHAT IT TAKES

The next hurdle, after committing to something as you figure out what you want to do, is to make sure your expectations are realistic. Some people want to train briefly and then earn six figures for a twenty-hour work week. I am not aware of any job training that can lead to that. And they don't want just any job. They want it to be white collar, not blue collar—but they do not want to commit to years of education for either.

When you manage your expectations and do what it takes to attain something better, you can accomplish much. I knew a home health aide who concluded that she was doing much of the hard work while a nurse, for far greater pay, would just briefly check on the patients and move on. She decided to go to nursing school while holding on to her home health aide job. She was considerably older than the typical nursing student, and she became an inspiration and motivator to her classmates. She told them her story and counseled them to get their education if they did not want to be left feeling someday that they do all the work while someone else gets the pay. Her life story encouraged the faltering and uncertain students to study harder to get through the nursing program.

I recently spent a few months in Maine doing financial consulting for Air National Guard members. In separate conversations, a couple of those clients told me how hard it was to find an electrician in that area. And when you could find one, their prices were rising—a quite natural consequence of supply and demand. If not enough people learn the trades, sooner or later there will be shortages. One mother, who worked as a nurse, told me with concern that her son wanted to be a plumber. I reminded her how much plumbing bills cost these days, and she remembered the plumbing bill she had to pay two years previously. Tradesmen can and do make excellent money.

QUESTIONS TO PONDER

Do you have the time, energy, and commitment to go to college or a trade school? Examine the job market in your area to learn what will work best for you. Make sure your family obligations will not prevent you from acquiring or enhancing work skills. If you cannot get to a classroom, you can find online educational resources and programs. Some employers are willing to pay much of the college bill, so find out whether your job offers such a benefit.

What do you do during your free time? Could you earn extra money in the holiday season? Seasonal job opportunities, such as delivery services, often come up. You can make more money, but it might not be an easy decision to be spending less time with your children and your family. It will depend on what you are willing and prepared to do.

I knew a single mother of a two-year-old who talked about her educational options. Her motherhood obligations were holding her back. "When is it ever going to get better?" I asked her. "Can you afford to wait until the child is twelve or thirteen for you to go back to school?" She felt trapped, and when you feel that way, none of your options seem like good ones. It feels like a choice between bad and worse. You wonder if there is a light at the end of the tunnel, but so long as you are moving along the tracks, you will make it out of the darkness. I worked with this young woman on a plan to obtain flexible employment so that she could attend college while working as needed. It would require sacrifice, but it could be done.

How much would you sacrifice? If you feel caught in such a cycle, what are you prepared to do? Ask yourself how you got into that situation. Examine your life decisions, circumstances, and beliefs that led to where you are now. By honestly assessing how your life has unfolded, you stand a much better chance of rising to new heights and financial freedom instead of being trapped in a cycle of financial failure for you and your family.

THE BOTTOM LINE

Some people have difficulty saving and investing in their future, not because they are overspending but because they truly need more income. Perhaps you are waiting for your dream job—but in the meantime, you must do what it takes to boost your salary while planning how to develop the career you envision.

CHAPTER 14

PREPARING FOR EDUCATION EXPENSE

To everything there is a season, and a time to every purpose under the heaven: a time to be born, and a time to die; a time to plant, and a time to pluck up that which is planted.

—Ecclesiastes 3:1,2

Now that your baby has graduated from high school, what next? If he or she chooses to go to college or trade school, are you ready to pay the cost? Do you see that as your responsibility? Many parents want to help with those expenses, but it is important that they find the right balance and not sacrifice the money that they should be setting aside for retirement.

In this chapter, we will look at how to prepare to pay for a college or trade school education. This is the season for planting the seeds that will produce the harvest. This is the time when a young person will be learning, growing, preparing. First we will ask the big question of *whether* you should prepare, as some parents strongly believe that their children should find their own way. But if you do intend to send your children to school, what can you afford?

As a personal financial advisor, the first thing I would tell parents is that this is not their priority. Preparing for your children's educational expenses should not be at the top of your list. Your priority should be preparing for your retirement. That is not to say that you should not be concerned about those educational expenses. I am saying that unless you can adequately do both, your retirement needs to come first.

Consider the risk involved in planning for your child's education. That's right, risk. Remember that most anything we do involves risk, and we need to identify and prepare for it. The risk of preparing for your child's education is that he or she may decide not to go to school. How will you feel if your child does not share your vision or seemingly does not appreciate your sacrifice? Perhaps your son or daughter will be determined to see the world by joining the service, getting technical skills there. If you have targeted money specifically for a college education, that investment could be sidetracked, just as it could be if your child got a full scholarship.

PUBLIC, PRIVATE, OR FOR-PROFIT?

If your child does decide to go to college, the big question will be where. For example, will it be a for-profit college or a state-sponsored college? I view the for-profit colleges with suspicion. They are under a tremendous amount of pressure to put profits over what is best for the students, and I believe some of them water down their educational standards as a result. Often the credits earned there will not transfer to other colleges.

I recently advised a client not to allow her son to go to a for-profit school that I believe has a shaky reputation. I pointed out that he could apply for the same program at a city university for half the price and without a loan. I later learned that he attended for one semester anyway and then dropped out—but still had to begin paying back his student loan.

The cost of going to a for-profit school is often two or three times the cost of going to a state-sponsored university or a community college. However, some for-profit schools do offer great programs that can be in your child's best interest. If you go that route, just be sure that you and your child are choosing one of the good ones.

Another consideration is whether to choose a public or a private college. Private colleges tend to be much more expensive, so why pay more if your salary will not depend on where you got your degree? Few jobs pay extra just because your degree was from a private college. However, some students and their parents are willing to pay more, and have the resources to do so, for what they perceive to be a better college experience. That is a different discussion. It comes down to what you want to buy. Are you paying just for the degree, or are you paying for that experience as well? Perhaps you are willing to pay for an Ivy League experience at a prestigious "name" school even though one with a less lofty reputation would provide a solid education—except without the luxurious dorms and gourmet chefs.

IN SEARCH OF SCHOLARSHIPS

Educational inflation has made it exceedingly difficult to put oneself through school by holding a part-time job, which many students once did at state- and city-sponsored schools. They increasingly look for financial aid and scholarship opportunities to fill the gap.

As you consider better options to support your children, encourage them to find outside scholarships. The student may qualify for a number of small scholarships that pay $500 to $1,000.

Your employer, union, association, or bank may offer scholarships. You may find scholarships related to your child's activities or field of interest, such as sports, journalism, politics, volunteerism, and so on.

Online websites and search engines have made it much easier to track down such resources. It still takes time and effort, but it can be done. A lot of people look for the one big scholarship that will pay it all, but a smart approach is also to cobble together some of those smaller ones that many students overlook or consider too small for the effort. Remember, though, that ten $1,000 scholarships that are easier to obtain will pay for the same expenses as one $10,000 scholarship that is harder to obtain.

Encourage your children to be active in something. Not only will the activity keep them occupied, they might also earn a tuition-free scholarship to the college of their choice. Speak with the high school and college guidance counselors for more information. It takes work and time to uncover opportunities, so start early while your child is in middle school, and be careful about application deadlines. Document all the opportunities discovered, whether big or small. With enough time and preparation, your child could secure a scholarship or scholarships that will help greatly in coping with the financial challenge of paying for higher education.

INVESTMENT STRATEGIES

If you have made up your mind to prepare for your child's education, think twice before placing investments in the name of your child. If you do, your child could get less financial aid as a result when the college puts together a package. You also should seek out tax advice on how to handle these assets so that you can maximize the potential savings.

A 529 savings plan could be a good way to invest for future college expenses. It allows you to grow your money free of federal tax, and often state tax, if it is to be used for educational purposes. If it is not used for education, however, you must pay those taxes, plus an additional 10 percent surcharge on the money taken out. Also be aware that the money in this account could influence the size of a needs-based financial aid package that the school puts together.

Saving money in a Roth IRA (in the parents' name, not the child's) can be a better option to pay for education, so long as doing so does not compromise retirement plans. As we discussed in chapter 10 on retirement planning, you do not get tax savings when you put money into a Roth, but later you can withdraw from it tax-free. The advantage is that you do not have to use the money for college. If your child receives scholarships and aid packages that cover the total cost of school, the money in the Roth can be used for something else. In addition, the money in a Roth does not affect the amount of needs-based financial aid, in contrast to a 529 savings plan.

In addition, a variety of other savings and investment instruments with names such as UGMAs and UTMAs and Coverdell accounts could be useful for funding an education, depending on the family situation and objectives. They have both pros and cons, and I cannot advise which of those, if any, would be appropriate for you without getting to know you and the full extent of your finances. Just know that, when it comes to paying for college, there are a number of investment vehicles that you can use.

As you can see, there are a number of issues to consider. That is why I highly recommend that you have a discussion with a professional to discuss your financial situation. No book can fully analyze your unique financial situation and tailor a financial plan for you.

SHOULD YOU TAKE OUT A LOAN?

Should you take out a loan to help pay for your children's education? That can be a touchy subject. On one hand, you feel that you should do everything you can to help, and you do not want your children to think you are not supporting their ambitions. On the other hand, a college loan comes with risks. You are responsible for it even if your child does not complete college, and that holds true whether you cosigned the loan or are solely responsible for it. If your child should pass away, God forbid, you are still on the hook for that loan. If you do not pay, even your Social Security check and various retirement accounts could be garnished. Remember, again, that everything has a risk—and that is what you could face here.

If you do decide to take out a loan, you must accept that you are now partners in this venture. You could be a truly silent partner and allow your child to make the educational decisions or a domineering partner who must approve every move. Or you could try a collaborative relationship. In any case, you should be keenly aware of what your child is studying. Is the academic program preparing your child for employment in this economic environment? You do not want to overpay for a degree that could be attained more cheaply and provide the same income potential.

Examine your risks. Carefully consider how taking out a loan for your child's college expenses will impact your own finances and retirement plans. Whatever you decide, be prepared to live with the consequences of your decision. What are your options if your child squanders your sacrifice? What will happen if your child cannot or will not help pay the bill? Keep in mind that if you say no to a loan and let your child be responsible for those costs, you are teaching personal responsibility.

A couple who are dear friends of mine, Steven and Sally, are raising their son to understand that he will be 100 percent responsible for his own education. They will tell him that in no uncertain terms as he grows up. What he won't be told is that mom and dad are saving so that one day he will have a great down payment on a house or seed money for a business venture. If he does find out about that plan, they figure he will be even more motivated to get a good education and strive to do well in life so that he will merit such a gift. With their outside savings for their son, Steven and Sally are keeping the options open.

THE BOTTOM LINE

Like many parents, you may wish to make sure your children have the financial resources for college tuition and expenses. There are many options, including scholarships, financial aid, and savings instruments. You must take care, however, that paying for the children's college costs does not mean you are sacrificing what you should be saving for retirement. Choose the college wisely, and know what you are paying for.

CHAPTER 15

TEACHING YOUR KIDS

Train up a child in the way he should go: and when he is old, he will not depart from it.

—Proverbs 22:6

A major reason so many people have problems with their finances today is that they did not learn the important principles during childhood. Instead, they observed patterns and developed habits that were destructive, and those habits were not corrected.

Ask yourself whether you were raised to learn the importance of budgeting and spending cautiously. Was that what was modeled to you? Or did you see your parents go deeply into debt to buy a new car or go on a fancy vacation?

I fully know that my life would have been different if the right lessons had been taught to me at an early age. If you feel that way too, imagine the difference that good financial teaching might have made in your life. If the power of compounding and time had been demonstrated to you and you had been encouraged to take advantage of it, what would your finances look like now? If someone had clearly shown you that you do not need a lot of money to make money, despite the lies to the contrary, how would that knowledge influence your financial accomplishments today?

Those who do not learn early to save and invest are less likely to do so later—even if they are making a lot of money. Some households with six-figure incomes struggle financially. Even if your child earns a significant amount, that success is at risk if he or she does not learn how to save and grow that money. Young people need to learn important money habits now. They should be learning key elements of saving, budgeting, and investing from you.

You can be the model of good finances to your own children and to those around you. Children do pick up behaviors and attitudes from their parents, whether we recognize it or not. Think about all those old expressions, some of which you may have used yourself: "like father, like son," "like mother, like daughter," "the apple doesn't fall far from the tree," "a chip off the old block." I'm sure you have known people who exhibit qualities that reflect those of their parents. People often come to see life—and finances—in much the same way as their parents. What financial behaviors are your children picking up from you? What financial lessons are you imparting to them?

LESSONS FOR VARIOUS AGE GROUPS

You can find many resources on effective ways to teach finances to children of various ages. Here are just a few of the books and other materials that I would recommend. You can read these together and talk about the lessons that they impart:

- *The Berenstain Bears' Dollars and Sense*, by Stan and Jan Berenstain. This book, for children ages three to seven, teaches fundamentals of money management as Brother and Sister Bear take responsibility for their allowances. The book includes a series of tear-out checks that children can use to track where their money goes.

- *The Lemonade War*, by Jacqueline Davies. In this book, for ages seven to ten, brother and sister Evan and Jessie compete to make the most money over the summer with their separate lemonade stands, and in the process they learn something not only about managing money but also about getting along in life.
- *The Motley Fool Investment Guide for Teens: 8 Steps to Having More Money Than Your Parents Ever Dreamed Of*, by David and Tom Gardner. The well-known founders of the Motley Fool multimedia investment company turn to an adolescent audience as they share their investment wisdom.

ACTIVITIES FOR VARIOUS AGE GROUPS

To get started now, here are some ideas to help your children learn the fundamentals. These are nothing new, and you can find many variations online, but generally they work like this:

- For younger children, up to about age eight, set up money management jars. Give each child three jars in which to distribute the money received from an allowance, from chores, or as gifts. In one of the jars, the child will put money for spending on things that he or she wants now. In another, the child will put money for things desired later. In the third, the "giving jar," the child can put money to donate to a church or use to help someone. The parent can provide appropriate guidance on how much goes into which jar, but the child should learn the consequences of his or her own decisions.

- Children eight and older need to learn the power of their financial choices. You might give the child five dollars and point out that the money has the power to purchase only so many things. The child must pick and choose, learning that money is not infinite and that buying one thing will prevent the purchase of another thing. In other words, you must make choices in life.
- In the teenage years, young people can learn to work out a household budget, identifying the range of expenses and how much money each will require. That awareness will serve them well as they head out into the world and set up their own households. You may want to talk about how your own household is run. You need to pay the rent or mortgage, for example. You need to pay for electricity and gas. You need to pay for toilet paper. Encourage the teen to add other line items to the list and work out a budget, and ask whether he or she could imagine living without any of those things. Explain that they all come at a cost.

TALKING TO YOUR ADULT CHILDREN

A lot of parents don't talk to their kids about money matters. As a young person, I never heard a word about the cost of setting up a household. What are you going to do if the average rent in the area is $1,000 a month, or $12,000 a year, and you get a job offer that will bring you $20,000 after taxes? Could you possibly survive on that? Seeing that big picture in advance may help a young person narrow his or her career choices to ones that are sufficient to pay the bills. Either that or they will recognize that their lifestyle will have to accommodate their career choice.

If your children have grown to adulthood, it is high time to have open and honest conversations with them. It is never too late. Why not invite them over for a home-cooked meal so that you can bring up the issue of saving and investing? You can share with them what you have learned by reading this very book—and perhaps how you feel you fell short in preparing them with the right tools to grow their finances.

This could also be an opportunity to talk to your children about retirement planning. If you feel uncertain about whether you have saved sufficiently, share those concerns. If you regret that you did not take certain steps when you were younger, tell them what you would have done differently. As a Christian you fully understand the power of testimony. Sharing these thoughts can have a profound impact.

Point out the real-life decisions that you made and their consequences. Your children can learn not only from what you did right but also from what you did wrong. Remind them that they, too, will need to save and invest effectively for retirement. When you honestly share with your children the issues that you face and how you are coping, they are likely to fill you in on their own preparations for this crucial stage of life.

THE BOTTOM LINE

As a parent, you have a responsibility to encourage your children to be more financially aware. You can help them learn important lessons about money by providing materials and engaging in activities appropriate to their age, and you can share with them your own experiences. They need to learn how to set up a budget and live within it.

CHAPTER 16

PROTECTING YOUR FAMILY, YOUR MONEY

Thus saith the Lord: 'Set thine house in order, for thou shalt die and not live.'

—Isaiah 38:1

We must prepare for our passing. "It is appointed unto men once to die," we read in Hebrews 9:27. The Lord warned Hezekiah to get his house in order because he was facing death. We must be mindful that life on earth goes on for others after our passing. For every household, an orderly process is essential.

If you pass away without your house in order, your family could fall into disarray. It has happened often. I have heard people tell of the devastation that poor planning can cause among brothers and sisters. Relatives may stop speaking to one another. They may fight over the death certificate to gain access to the deceased's bank accounts, whether for the right reasons or the wrong ones. Some who have seen such strife among others end up repeating it in their own families. Ask yourself this: If you were to die today, would your affairs be handled in an orderly manner without causing strife and division?

In this chapter, we will look at some of the basics of what you should set up for your estate and end-of-life planning. Your life circumstances will determine the details, but this will give you an idea of what the minimums should be.

LIFE INSURANCE

The principle goal of life insurance is this: when you pass away, your family will receive a death benefit, with the amount dependent on how much insurance you purchase. The amount of insurance that is appropriate for you and your family will depend on a variety of factors.

At a minimum, you need enough insurance to cover your burial costs. Many families, at the time they are trying to cope with the death of a loved one, are also struggling to pay the funeral costs. Are you putting your family in that situation? Is a loved one placing you in that situation? In addition, the family may be struggling with much more than burial expenses, such as how to survive without the income that you provided while you were alive and working. If someone depends on your paycheck, you may wish to purchase at least enough additional insurance to cover a year's worth of your income. That will buy time for your dependents to adjust financially to your parting.

Many people fail to plan for their life insurance needs for this simple reason: they do not want to contemplate their own death. In their twenties, they often feel as if they will be young and strong forever, and that is why they put off planning for retirement. It is hard to imagine at that age that life insurance might be needed one day. And as you age, you do not want to deal with such a thought.

You have two basic choices—term life insurance and permanent life insurance—when choosing the coverage that is best for you and your family. Term policies generally are less expensive than permanent policies.

- Term insurance covers you for a specific period, during which you make premium payments. After that period, the coverage ends. If you purchase a thirty-year term policy for a $100,000 death benefit, for example, your beneficiary will get that much if you keep up your payments and die within that period. If you die thirty years and one day later, your beneficiary will get nothing from the insurance company.
- Permanent insurance is not limited to a term. As long as you keep making the payments, the policy will pay out when you pass away. Though these policies cost more, you can know that no matter how long you live, your family will get some funds to pay for your burial expenses and, depending on the size of your policy, for their other financial needs.

You should decide on a life insurance policy as soon as possible, while you are relatively young. The state of your health will have much to do with whether you are considered insurable. Some people do not wake up to the need to acquire life insurance until they have had a health crisis, such as a heart attack. At that point, a policy could become unaffordable or unavailable. In general, women are considered to be more insurable than men, based on longevity statistics, but your health history plays a key role in whether you can get insurance and how much it will cost.

A WILL

Your last will and testament is another important element in protecting your family and your financial legacy. Your will outlines what you want done with your property, money, and possessions when you pass away. If you have dependent minor children, you can name who will become their guardian. Your will also names your executor, who will ensure that your final instructions are carried out.

The specific terms of your will can prevent a lot of family infighting. If you have items of importance that you truly want to get to specific people, your will can make that crystal clear for all your heirs. I once spoke with a man whose grandfather, who had a family-owned funeral parlor, died without a will. The four siblings could not come to an agreement. After the dust settled, they ended up splitting the estate at a reduced amount—the lawyers got the rest. To continue operating the business, the grandson had to buy back the very same property that housed the funeral parlor. That scenario could have been avoided if a carefully worded will had been in place.

LONG-TERM CARE

Our bodies inevitably age, and we confront various ailments. Some people want to stay in their home, but doing so will require not only physical changes to the home but also enough money to pay for a home health aide for help with day-to-day activities.

You must consider the risk that you will need to enter a nursing-care facility. If you are currently in good health, you can get an idea of whether you might need that service someday by looking at your family's history. In some families, old people are relatively capable till the end. In others, they tend to linger and need a lot of medical support. You could be the exception to any such trend, of course, but it does give you a perspective on the probabilities.

You can take out an insurance policy to help cover these potential expenses, or you can save money on your own to pay for them. Either approach requires careful advance planning, and you can use a number of strategies or a combination. Besides traditional long-term care insurance, you could look into one of the hybrid life insurance policies or annuities that will pay a portion of the death benefit in advance if it is needed for long-term care.

One strategy that some people use to qualify for Medicaid coverage of their long-term care needs is to put all their money into a trust or transfer it to the children, and as long as they do that at least five years in advance, it is considered a legitimate maneuver. In whatever way you decide to cover that risk, you should make your plans well in advance. Otherwise, the cost of long-term care could consume much of what you spent a lifetime accumulating. As you make these decisions, you should be working with a professional who can get to know you personally and understand your needs and your goals.

LIVING WILL / HEALTH CARE PROXY

Another important document to consider is often called a "living will" or advance health care directive. It describes the extent of life-sustaining treatment that you want in your final days. Some people would like the doctors to do everything they can to prolong life. Others want one shot at revival, and that's it. You may or may not want the doctors to use a feeding tube and assisted breathing to maintain your life. You may believe strongly in death with dignity. A living will helps you to meet the maker on your terms.

Family sometimes can be divided over the best course of medical care for a loved one. You can prevent the possibility that your loved ones will end up in court, fighting over you, by legally appointing who will have the final say. You are doing the loving thing for your family by deciding that in advance, as is also the case when you draft a living will. You are showing your family that you care enough about them that you want your wishes known clearly so that they will not be in a state of doubt.

POWER OF ATTORNEY

Depending on your assets, your family structure, and your family dynamics, you may wish to designate someone with the power of attorney to make all or limited decisions on your behalf. You are authorizing that person to work on your behalf. There are two broad types: durable power of attorney and a limited power of attorney.

The durable power of attorney for legal and financial matters authorizes someone of your choosing to act on your behalf if you cannot. That person generally will have the discretion to invest or spend your assets, although you can specify that those powers be limited. It is called a durable power because it continues for as long as you cannot make your own decisions and take your own actions. It does not continue after you die, though.

A limited power of attorney clearly outlines what the person can and cannot do on your behalf. For an example, you may give someone the power just to oversee your business ventures and make the decisions to keep your business going in an orderly fashion.

No matter your situation, there is a way to design a power of attorney that will work best for you. Just make sure you get professional assistance, especially if you have some unclear or special circumstances that you want addressed.

BENEFICIARY DESIGNATIONS

Make sure that your listed beneficiaries are up-to-date on all your financial documents, including retirement plans and insurance policies. Let's say you never updated your 401(k) plan after opening your account two decades ago, and it still lists your ex-spouse as the beneficiary. If you die, he or she will be entitled to all that money, even if you have remarried. Your heirs cannot say you forgot to make that change. The beneficiary listing is legally binding.

In working with clients, I make it a practice to regularly review those beneficiary designations and ensure that they are accurate and up-to-date. The beneficiary designations, and other titled documents such as the deed to your house, will supersede any last wishes that you decree in your will or in a trust, so it is essential that you know to whom you are leaving the money.

TRUSTS

As another step in protecting your family, you may wish to set up a trust. Trusts are not just for highly affluent people who need a way to protect their assets from the estate tax. A properly drafted trust can provide legal protection from lawsuits and creditors, and you can include provisions in a trust that will specify exactly who will get what and place limits on how the recipients can spend it.

After your attorney drafts a trust for you and you place assets in it, you get to say how the money will be used. For example, you might want to leave only a small percentage annually to the children or give them only the interest earned but none of the principal. You could limit the use of that money to educational expenses, the purchase of a home, or the cost of establishing a business, as just a few examples. Maybe you want to protect your life's work from the excesses of a spendthrift child, or maybe you want to make sure that a child with special needs receives lifelong care.

You cannot stipulate such things through the terms of your will, nor do you have such control with the beneficiary designation. A trust is the only way that you can set up such provisions that will continue to protect and benefit your family, even after you are long gone.

THE BOTTOM LINE

For the sake of protecting your family and all that you have worked so hard to attain, you should attend to matters of insurance, long-term care planning, and estate planning. A comprehensive planner can help you fit the pieces of the puzzle into place.

CHAPTER 17

WHY YOU NEED FINANCIAL HELP

Without counsel purposes are disappointed: but in the multitude of counsellors they are established.

—Proverbs 15:22

In the Parable of the Talents, Jesus told of a wealthy man who, before traveling to a far country, entrusted his money to three servants. To the first he left five bags of gold, to the second he left two bags, and to the third he left one bag. The first servant invested the money and doubled the holdings, as did the second servant. The third hid the bag of gold by burying it. Upon his return, the traveler praised and rewarded the first two servants but condemned the third for not having deposited the gold with bankers to earn interest. He ordered that the "wicked and slothful" servant be thrown into the darkness, where there would be "weeping and gnashing of teeth."

It's pretty clear, isn't it? If you are unsure what to do with your money, or if you lack the time or inclination to manage it well, do not just hide it away or stuff it in your mattress. Instead, seek out professional help to grow that money into something greater.

Do not let the stories about crooks like Bernie Madoff turn you off to working with a financial advisor. So much attention goes to a few bad people who have tarnished the industry. Meanwhile, countless professionals work hard every day, with honesty and passion, to help people reach their financial goals.

COMMISSIONS AND FEES

For many people, an insurance salesperson is their first contact with the financial services industry. Insurance salespeople generally work on commission, and that has led many people to become skeptical about the entire industry. Don't get me wrong: insurance is highly important, and most agents are reputable. It is an essential industry—but it is based on a model in which the agents are not compensated unless you buy something.

That model of compensation raises the risk of misbehaviors within the industry. It is not uncommon for people to be sold policies that are unsuitable for their situations. Sometimes they are offered policies that they cannot afford to maintain. They have other liabilities that should have been addressed first.

Fundamentally, I do not have a problem with commission-based financial services when they are offered by professionals who truly care about their clients. Many financial advisors are commission based as well, and many of them also do a great job. As a client, however, you may be left wondering whether you are getting a recommendation that is best for you or best for the planner. Such doubts can be unnerving, especially for first-time investors.

Some financial planners—myself included—are fee based. They charge a fee, generally a percent or two of the amount of your money under management. But if you had only $2,000 to manage, how practical would it be for the planner to help you when that fee would amount to only $40 or so? As you can see, their incentive is to work with people who have already built up significant assets. You may instead be looking for someone to help get you to that point. Many fee-based planners will not want to work with you if you do not have enough money. However, unlike most planners, I am willing to work with you and assist you in growing your finances and assets.

Other planners charge by the hour. This type of planning can also pose problems. If you schedule an hour-long appointment and are missing some key documents, you still must pay for that hour. Some planning processes can take many hours to complete; if you are facing some complicated issues, all those hours can add up to an expensive proposition.

Your other choice for financial planning is the do-it-yourself option. You do not have to worry about conflicts of interest, or being offered a product that is not best for you, and you can avoid the various types of payment structures. However, there is still a risk. You don't know what you don't know. You will need time and patience to learn the various aspects of finances and investments. Are you prepared for all that work? Remember, once again, everything has a risk. The key is to find the level of risk you feel comfortable with.

I should mention one more option, one that most people follow: you can do absolutely nothing. A few people have done well with that option. A great many others have not—and in the recent financial climate, success has been particularly unlikely for those who do nothing. Do not risk the weeping and gnashing of teeth.

WHEN TO SEE A PLANNER

Everyone can benefit from seeing a planner at four pivotal points in their lives:

- **Early to midtwenties.** Hopefully you have finished your education and are settling into your first job. A planner can help you identify life goals and find a strategy to meet them. You will get a sense of how much you need to save and what type of investment mix would be best for you.

- **At forty.** You are in your middle years and need to take stock of where you are financially. You should examine how closely you have followed the financial plan you laid out fifteen years earlier. You can adjust your investment style and how much you are saving.

- **At fifty-five.** You are nearing the finish line but can make adjustments. This is a crucial time to address any family dynamics with financial implications. A major financial crisis will have a severe impact on your plans for retirement. Health issues start to come into play. You should start thinking about retirement needs and other priorities.

- **At sixty-two to sixty-five** (at least a year or two before you retire). You want to take final stock and have a financial outline of your retirement years in place. Estate and legacy issues need to be examined.

HOW A GOOD PLANNER CAN HELP YOU

- **Adding financial value.** A Morningstar study showed that financial planners can add, on average, 2 percent to people's investments.[4] A study by ING found that people who work with financial advisors are able to save and grow more money, leading to more money in retirement.[5] In other words, the service pays for itself.

- **Saving you money.** When the market crashed in late 2007 and early 2008, many people bailed out when they should have been bailing in. Within eight years, the market had doubled, but many people waited too long to jump back in. Those who made that mistake could have benefited immensely from good advice. It would have cost a small fraction of the amount they could have gained.
- **Keeping you on track.** A lot of good ideas end up sitting on a shelf. A plan is no good unless it is put to use and followed. A planner will help to keep your strategies in motion and prevent you from veering very far away from your financial goals.
- **Suggesting good investments.** Your advisor will be able to point out moneymaking opportunities. It is in your advisor's own best interest to ensure the best possible financial experience for you. If you are a client, you will benefit from that expertise.
- **Setting priorities.** What is the best course of action to help you achieve your goals? A planner can help you decide where to focus first.

---

4 David Blanchett and Paul Kaplan, "Alpha, Beta, and Now ... Gamma," Morningstar, accessed May 19, 2017, https://corporate1.morningstar.com/uploadedFiles/US/AlphaBetaandNowGamma.pdf.

5 "Advisor Value," Voya, accessed May 19, 2017, http://forprofessionals.voya.com/sites/forprofessionals.voya.com/files/3024666.X.G-2_AdvisorValue_WhitePaper_19855_FINAL.pdf

- **Adjusting to major life events.** Life takes many turns, some unexpected and expensive, and you may need to review your asset allocation, change how much you invest, or take on a bit more risk.
- **Setting realistic expectations.** A would-be investor told me he wanted to turn $3,000 into $10,000 by the end of the year. I told him it could be done—but the odds were low, it would be highly risky, and he might lose it all. He changed his mind. You need a steady hand, especially when the market is falling.
- **Transitioning into retirement.** A planner can help you to navigate the many financial and lifestyle considerations during this phase of your life.
- **Creating an estate plan.** As you are deciding how to distribute your assets to the next generation, you need professional help with the documents and the details, including the tax considerations.
- **Custom designing.** Financial planning is for everyone, whether you are rich, poor, or somewhere in the middle. You need a plan that is tailored to your specific situation. If you fail to plan, you are planning to fail.
- **Seeing the whole picture.** You need to understand how the various elements of your financial situation affect one another. I met a woman whose lawyer had given her sound advice on a legal matter, but she had not considered the tax consequences. If she had planned comprehensively, she could have reduced a $50,000 bill from the IRS.

- **Providing peace of mind.** People who work with a planner feel more confident as they head into their retirement years. They save time and energy not having to worry about all the ups and downs of the market.

WHOM SHOULD YOU CHOOSE?

As you consider your options, my recommendation is that you look for a fee-only CERTIFIED FINANCIAL PLANNER™ practitioner. Although you must get to know the individual, as in choosing any professional, this designation indicates that the advisor has had training and education with an emphasis on comprehensive financial planning.

CFP® practitioners design plans that consider the entire life situation and all the needs of their clients. It's a balanced approach. It's like making sure you get a well-rounded meal. As is evident in this book, I believe in truly comprehensive financial planning—I understand there are financial and emotional considerations that have to be taken into account in developing a plan.

CFP® practitioners also abide by the "fiduciary" standard set by the CFP® Board. Fiduciaries are ethically and legally bound to place your interest first. They are to fully disclose any and all conflicts of interest and potential conflicts of interest to you. If you have any doubts or concerns, simply request that you have a fiduciary relationship with the planner, and ask that it be clearly stated in writing.

I suggest that you first pay the advisor solely for the service of creating a comprehensive financial plan, after which the relationship would be over—unless you decide to continue with a separate contract for further assistance in putting the plan into action. You and the planner would then work out the fee arrangements.

The advantage of that approach is that you potentially could implement the plan yourself or hire a different advisor. You are not tied to the one who created the plan, and that helps to remove any doubts that the advice might be self-serving. After I help people design their plans, they need not feel an obligation to stay with me. Unless they want to form a relationship for life, my job is done. I'm here to help people, not capture them. We need to be a good fit.

How important is this to you? Read again the list of benefits of working with a financial planner. I once encouraged a young man to meet with a financial planner before marrying. He and his fiancée did not find the time or money to do so—and therefore they had to pay an additional $8,000 in taxes, an expense they could have avoided. I'm sure you have heard the expression "penny wise, pound foolish." Is that going to be you?

You stand to gain value, savings, and financial direction by developing a personalized financial plan. Remember, people find the money for things that matter to them and for the things that they feel and believe are necessary. This is your financial future we are talking about. And not just yours—the future success of your family and the Lord's work is dependent on you having a strong financial foundation. Does this matter to you? Do you believe and feel that this is necessary?

You have come so close. Do not falter now. Even if you think that all is well, it is worth the time and the expense to consult a professional. If you hear that you are in good shape, you have not wasted your money any more than when a doctor tells you all is well after a checkup. The doctor also might tell you that you need to change some habits before it's too late. Your financial planner does the same thing about your finances.

THE BOTTOM LINE

There is much to consider when choosing who will be your financial advisor. How is that person compensated? When should you look for help? What are the qualities that you should seek? You need to make sure that you are a good fit. This should be a relationship for life. Above all, you need to have a financial plan.

CONCLUSION

TO WHOM MUCH IS GIVEN . . .

But wilt thou know, O vain man, that faith without works is dead?

—James 2:20

This is where it all comes together. You are at the crossroads of action or inaction. Which will you choose? Will you follow through on all that you have learned, or will you fall back to your old ways?

"Therefore to him that knoweth to do good, and doeth it not, to him it is sin," we read in James 4:17. You have just finished a book, based on Scripture, about how to get your finances in order so that you might be more of a blessing to the Lord, to your church, to your household. No longer can you fall back on the excuse of ignorance. You know how to do good. You possess the knowledge—and as we read in Luke 12:48, "unto whomsoever much is given, of him shall be much required."

The church has always needed the support of those with financial resources. In Corinth, for example, when Paul was laboring to build the church there, his financial backing came from the church in

Macedonia, which had the wherewithal to support his missionary work. The Philippi congregation clearly included members with the ability to advance God's work both at home and abroad. Then, as now, the church needs money to spread the gospel. The church needs mighty men and women of wealth to empower the ministry to go forth.

Who knows what the Lord will call you to do in ten years or in twenty years. He may ask you to support or start a ministry. Will you be ready? You cannot simply smile and say that the Lord will make a way. He does, but he still expects the farmers to farm and the shepherds to protect their flock. God was with David, but David still had to fight off the lion with his own hands. The farmer and the shepherd must do their part. So must you.

CLOSING REMARKS

I would to thank you for taking the time to read this book. I pray to our Heavenly Father that you have been inspired to take charge of your financial life. Take the next step right now and "harden not your hearts, as in the provocation" (Hebrews 3:8). Don't say, "I will do it tomorrow," or get distracted by day-to-day life events. Connect now by following and liking me on Facebook at @PathToAbundantLiving. By connecting you will receive timely financial suggestions, ideas, and encouragement that will empower you to stay on the Path To Abundant Living. You can be a further blessing to me and others by sharing your thoughts about the book and providing testimony to the challenges and power of financial readiness. If you are not a Facebook person then sign up for my newsletter at www.PathToAbundantLiving.com. You will receive financial planning thoughts, solutions, and support from time to time from me. Reach out and contact me if you, your organization, or your group would be interested in me presenting at your next event or gathering. Feel free to email me at PathToAbundantLiving@gmail.com for further information.

Printed in the USA
CPSIA information can be obtained
at www.ICGtesting.com
JSHW012053140824
68134JS00035B/3415

9 781599 328683